The Growth of a Storyteller

This sequel to the bestselling *Princesses, Dragons and Helicopter Stories* reveals the positive impact the storytelling and story acting curriculum of Vivian Gussin Paley has on young children's literacy, communication and confidence. Telling the story of three years of classroom-based research with children aged two to seven, it shows the Helicopter Stories approach in action, capturing the children's development as storytellers and their delight at having their stories listened to, scribed and acted out.

In each chapter Trisha Lee's passion for children's unique voices shines through as she shares and reflects on the children's stories, paying each of them the same respect as would normally be bestowed on adult writers. Exploring the importance of story in children's lives, the book:

- Examines the cognitive and developmental impact of implementing a Helicopter Stories approach over an extended time period

- Analyses the stories told by children using the story structure of the Hero's Journey, and the seven basic plot types

- Explores how and why stories connect with us including children's innate ability to empathise with the hero from a very young age

- Includes rich case studies of children at different ages and developmental stages including those with additional needs

Offering a fascinating insight into how Helicopter Stories work in practice and addressing the frequently asked questions about the benefits of using this approach, *The Growth of a Storyteller* is valuable reading for anyone interested in storytelling and story acting with their children.

Trisha Lee is a professionally trained theatre director and storyteller. Author of *Princesses, Dragons and Helicopter Stories*, she is passionate about the importance of storytelling and story acting in children's lives. In 2002 Trisha founded MakeBelieve Arts. She oversees development of the artistic programme; devising and directing theatre shows, developing and performing in The Poetry Basket and The Story Basket; and managing all aspects of MakeBelieve Arts Online Learning. Widely known for her work on Helicopter Stories, she is in demand to speak at conferences and to share her training via Helicopter Stories On Demand.

"Without imagination we are lost — from ourselves, the world and one another. This magical book is your map to the 'stories' of childhood and a timely reminder to dream harder, bigger and brighter. Your children need you to read it."

Greg Bottrill, *author of* Can I Go and Play Now —
Rethinking the Early Years, *and* School and the Magic of Children

"Trisha Lee's magical book, *The Growth of a Storyteller*, shows how the youngest children develop the ability to tell their own stories and act them out. Starting with two-year-olds, Trisha watched as they learned to expand their characters and plots, and she shows the reader why storytelling and story acting are such a valuable tool for the language development, social skills, and emotional well-being of all children."

Jane Katch, *author of* Under Deadman's Skin — Discovering the
Meaning of Children's Violent Play, They Don't Like Me — Lessons on
Bullying, *and* Far Away From the Tigers

"This beautiful book is utterly captivating and should come with a warning that meals will go unprepared and dogs will go unwalked once you start reading it. A story in itself, it delivers theory and practical information and provides compelling evidence for the importance of ensuring that children's voices are heard, and valued, now more than ever. I guarantee you will find yourself listening to children in a different way after reading this."

Kym Scott, *Early Years Consultant, founder of A Place To Learn*

"Human beings are a storying species, get us together with a group of friends and we will all tell our stories. Trisha's work, which is inspired by the wonderful Vivian Gussin Paley, explores what it means to be a young storyteller and how the essential skills of storytelling develop when nurtured by skilled and knowledgeable adults. A must-read for anyone who works with young children."

Ruth Swailes, *School Improvement Advisor, Curriculum
Developer. Nursery World Trainer of the Year 2021*

The Growth of a Storyteller

Helicopter Stories in Action

Trisha Lee

Routledge
Taylor & Francis Group

LONDON AND NEW YORK

Cover image: © Amie Taylor

First published 2023
by Routledge
4 Park Square, Milton Park, Abingdon, Oxon, OX14 4RN

and by Routledge
605 Third Avenue, New York, NY 10158

Routledge is an imprint of the Taylor & Francis Group, an informa business

British Library Cataloguing-in-Publication Data
A catalogue record for this book is available from the British Library

Library of Congress Cataloging-in-Publication Data
A catalog record has been requested for this book

ISBN: 978-0-367-75189-0 (hbk)
ISBN: 978-0-367-75191-3 (pbk)
ISBN: 978-1-003-16140-0 (ebk)

DOI: 10.4324/9781003161400

Typeset in Bembo
by Newgen Publishing UK

In loving memory of
Vivian Gussin Paley 1929–2019
My friend and mentor for over twenty years.
You are forever in my heart.

Original image courtesy of Yu-ching Huang

Contents

Foreword

By Elaine Bennett, Founder of Keeping the Early Years Unique

I can still remember my mum taking me to the library as a small child, in the days when you could only take out four books and no more. I can still remember the joy of pouring over the brightly coloured square boxes, flicking through the books. I can still remember the feel and the smell of those plastic sleeves that protected them – and the painstaking decision: "Which ones would I choose?" I can still remember our small two-bedroomed flat, my Sarah Kay decorated bedroom (if you know, you know) surrounded by shelves of Enid Blyton, Richard Scarry, traditional fairy tales, Aesop's fables, Beatrix Potter, Peter, Jane and Pat, the Mr Men, nursery rhymes and so many more. My mum was an avid reader (and still is). I can still remember her snuggled up in her favourite armchair lost in a book telling me "Ok – just let me finish this chapter." She passed this baton to me, reading to me every night and making up stories and listening to mine. I have attempted to pass this gift to my son, an avid gamer – now sixteen. I took him to join the library at six weeks old and was given his first card by a perplexed looking librarian. I hope one day he returns to reading and the joy of getting lost in the pages of a great book instead of a virtual world!

Aged seven, my teacher the wonderful Mrs O'Connor wrote in my report that I was the best storyteller. Aged nine, another teacher, Mr Turner, even used a story I wrote one weekend to form the basis of our class assembly about a land with no colour "Ruolocon" – cue some expressive dance to Cyndi Lauper's True Colours. I cannot explain the pride I felt seeing my story being brought to life. In essence this was Helicopter Stories in the KS2 classroom. I was an expert at making up stories and telling them to family members during long car trips. I am a storyteller. There are days when I tell my class a story. I have no idea where it is going quite often – but it always goes somewhere! On occasions I even get a round of applause at the end. A couple of years ago on a trip to the beach, with the midday sun beating down and a desperate need for shade, I found myself telling a story to sixty reception children about a pirate ship coming to shore, some even looked across the waves expecting to see one! Now as I train teachers, speak publicly and lead campaigns to defend childhood through Keeping Early Years Unique – even as I write this to you now – I am still telling my story, still engaging an audience, connecting with you. Storytelling isn't something we grow out of. It is always there, perhaps hidden away under the pressures of life, but always there. Somewhere. Trisha Lee inspires us to dig deep, brush away the dirt and dust and rediscover it.

There really has never been a time that stories have mattered more. There has never been a more important time to read this book. In many parts of the world, as Vivian Gussin Paley experienced in the USA and as Trisha experiences here in England, teachers are fighting education systems where adults have no time. No time to listen. Children have no time to speak, let alone tell their story. In a world changed forever, with a focus on catching children up (whatever that means) and lost learning (whatever that means) and where so much trauma has been lived, surely there can be nothing more important than making time to tune in, listen and "story" together. There has never been a more important time to focus on those powerful back and forth interactions that research shows make the difference to so much more than filling heads with vocabulary. There has never been a more important time to be fascinated, to respect and value the contributions of our children as they share their stories, their imagination, their reality, their lives.

At Friars Primary School and Nursery, we use Helicopter Stories (as well as the Story and Poetry Basket) in our nursery and reception classes. We see our children come alive when they tell their stories, whether it's a unicorn doing rainbow poops, or bad guys in helicopters blowing everything up, or perhaps mum making pasta in the kitchen. We see them grow a few centimetres taller with pride. Their stories matter. When we come together to act them out and celebrate them around our stage, we are telling the author that their voice matters. And what more powerful message could we be giving our children in today's world?

So, thank you Trisha for asking me to write this foreword and to share my story. I am humbled. I am inspired by you to keep listening and keep storying.

Thank you to the wonderful Vivian for her love, guidance, and bravery to do the right thing and the bright, shining light she has passed to Trisha.

Thank you to all of you for choosing to read this book – I promise it will move and inspire you.

And of course, to the "real" authors – those who share their stories with us in this book, and those in our care who inspire and motivate us to be brave, stand up and do what must be done.

Grab a coffee, get comfortable and enjoy.

Over to you Trisha.

Introduction
The Beginning

*"What is coming from the mouths of kindergarteners is often the truest truth, the unclut-
tered voice of the soul, and none of us can afford not to listen."*

Vivian Gussin Paley
(Personal correspondence with Nisha Ruparel-Sen)

DOI: 10.4324/9781003161400-1

At the start of any sequel, it is the author's job to summarise what has gone before and take the reader with them on a voyage into the next instalment.

The Growth of a Storyteller is a sequel. It tells of my Helicopter Stories journey over the past few years, the children I have met and the stories they have told me.

> At MakeBelieve Arts we call this work Helicopter Stories, after Vivian Gussin Paley's book, *The Boy Who Would Be a Helicopter* (1990). There are many other names for Storytelling and Story Acting that have been adopted around the world. I have heard it called Story Square, Story Play, Doing Stories, Dragonfly, the Storytelling Curriculum, Carpet Drama, Magic Carpet and numerous other titles. Whatever you name it, I believe that if you use it on a regular basis with a group of children, you will find yourself in the incredible position of letting imagination fly.
>
> (Lee, 2016, *Princesses, Dragons and Helicopter Stories*, p. 2)

By the time I published *Princesses, Dragons and Helicopter Stories* six years ago, I was lucky enough to have worked with hundreds of settings worldwide, delivering Helicopter Stories to children aged two to seven years old. However, as MakeBelieve Arts is a theatre and education charity, the number of sessions I did with any group of children varied from as low as a one-off visit with a group I would never meet again to a series of up to twelve sessions spread out over a three- or four-month period.

The benefit this gave me is that I got to work with a diverse range of children, thousands of them. I saw how they reacted to having their stories scribed and then acted out, and I witnessed the value of Storytelling and Story Acting in developing children's confidence and creativity. I also experienced the practices of a wide variety of settings and schools, from those that are play-based to those that deliver a more formal curriculum. This gave me an understanding of how Helicopter Stories can work in any school or setting. It also meant that I could confidently say that the approach resonated with every child I had ever met, regardless of where they live, their social background, whether they have English as an additional language or special educational needs. I believe that telling stories and acting them out is something that children instinctively understand. They react to Helicopter Stories intuitively, as if they have just been waiting to be asked.

But there were disadvantages to the way that I was working. Until 2017, I never had the opportunity to follow the same group of children over several years or see first-hand the development that occurs when a child engages in Storytelling and Story Acting over a longer timescale. For a while, this didn't matter. My aim was to empower Early Years Practitioners to deliver Helicopter Stories themselves rather than rely on me to run the sessions. As a result, I effectively made myself redundant after very few visits. On the positive side, the feedback from this way of working was incredible. I heard hundreds of anecdotes from teachers and nursery staff sharing the benefits they witness from using Helicopter Stories year after year with each new cohort of children in their setting. However, none of the feedback I received or the work I took part in explored what happened to children's stories as they moved through Preschool to Reception and on into Year 1 and Year 2. It was only when MakeBelieve Arts decided to focus all of our energies on Helicopter Stories that I realised I was losing out on the opportunity to reflect on these benefits. I spoke about my dilemma with the Ironmongers' Foundation, a charitable trust that has funded MakeBelieve Arts over many years. They agreed to support us to deliver Helicopter Stories with the same cohorts of children over a longer timeframe.

In September 2017, a primary school in Chippenham, Wiltshire, said yes to hosting this programme. I was welcomed by both their Reception and Year 1 teacher. Between 2017 and 2020, I worked closely with both teachers, team-teaching the delivery of Helicopter Stories on my regular visits to their classrooms, and inviting them to deliver the approach on the weeks I wasn't there. The agreement I had with the school was that every class I worked with would participate in Helicopter Stories at least once a week and that I could stay with the children as they moved from Reception to Year 1 to Year 2.

Once the Ironmongers funding was in place, I set about raising additional funds to work with two- to four-year-olds at one of the feeder pre-schools. I began delivering Helicopter Stories in the preschool from January 2018. I was even lucky enough to follow one cohort of children all the way from pre-school until the end of the spring term of their first year in Reception.

Unfortunately, the longitudinal study was put on hold in March 2020 due to the Covid-19 lockdowns. But I did get to spend the best part of three years with these wonderful children running Helicopter Stories sessions alongside the staff who support them. During that time, I regularly scribed stories for over one hundred children aged between two to seven years old.

When I reread the stories of the two- to seven-year-olds I've worked with, I find myself laughing at their humour, marvelling at the poetry of their language, admiring the unpredictable nature of their views on the world, and reliving the enjoyment they felt as their stories were acted out. Throughout this publication, I will share with you a selection of these stories as I track the growth of a storyteller. I will also discuss what I have learned and how this has confirmed my belief in the value of long-term engagement with Helicopter Stories and its benefits for children's creativity and language development. I have included case studies and anecdotes alongside scientific research on the power of story. Plus, in the final chapter, I get the chance to revisit some of the children I worked with, and find out their thoughts on the benefits of this work.

Whether you are new to Helicopter Stories or even if you are familiar with it, I hope this publication will demonstrate that by bringing all the elements of this incredible approach together, you will be in possession of a magical tool that fits perfectly into your setting, enhances the communication and literacy skills of your children, and quickly becomes the highlight of your day. My wish is, that by reading this book, you will relive my joy at scribing these stories and connect with my deep-seated admiration for the voices of these young storytellers. But I am also on a mission, and I hope it is one that I can inspire you to help me with. I want to give every two- to seven-year-old across the world the opportunity to have their stories listened to, scribed and acted out, exactly in the way Vivian Gussin Paley did in her kindergarten classroom. I am determined to get the message out there, that part of our work with young children is to recognise and celebrate their storytelling abilities. Alongside this, we need to ensure that this innate ability is properly nurtured and allowed to grow in every setting and Early Years classroom around the world.

Over the past five years I have been on a journey, and now I invite you to join me and witness for yourself the sophisticated thinking and inherent storytelling abilities that I have discovered on my travels. I have been lucky enough to see first-hand the confidence that Helicopter Stories has given to the children I work with, and it is my desire to shout about their achievements that has driven me to write this sequel.

When I first started the longitudinal study, I wondered if I should find someone else to evaluate the work. I am not an academic. I am a theatre practitioner. There have been moments in my career when I have doubted whether I am qualified to write about my findings. I shared these anxieties with Vivian Gussin Paley, the woman who developed Storytelling and Story Acting, or what I call Helicopter Stories. I knew she would understand. Throughout her lifetime, Vivian won numerous awards for her contribution to Early Childhood practice. She is referred to as an outstanding educator, an early childhood researcher and a thought-provoking writer. Her thirteen books were all based on her insightful observations of the events in her classroom. However, even now, she is still not given the full credit she deserves in some academic circles.

Here is Vivian's reply, in one of her letters to me.

Vivian Gussin Paley – Personal Correspondence

Your part of the story is very important. Yours comes to the subject as pure theater, an approach very close to my heart. Yet, most people are concerned that in order to sell our ideas, we must include the academic and assessment values alongside.

Your letters are a treasure to me. Your understanding of the children's dramatic instincts and your appreciation of their stories and commentary surpasses anyone else I know.

Having read Vivian's response, I knew I had to share this story myself. It will not be a study in the "academic" sense of the word. There will be no quantitative research, no formal tone or style, no endnotes, footnotes, index, or peer review. Instead, I will write from my heart and my experiences, telling the stories of the children I have met and my observations on how they grew as storytellers over the time I spent with them. The anecdotes I share will be drawn from the things they've said and the stories they've told. I will reflect on my observations and express how these have shaped my understanding about the power of story. There will be references to books, films, talks and philosophies that I have come across along the way, many of which I searched for out of a need to understand this thing we call "story." I share these in the hope that they will inspire you to dig deeper into the emerging science behind this fascinating topic that I can only scratch the surface of within this publication.

Throughout my life, I have been a passionate advocate for the rights of the child, fighting for their voices to be heard and their creativity valued. *The Growth of a Storyteller* builds on this ethos. It values the two-year-old, starting on his or her journey into the exhilarating world of words. It ends with the seven-year-old knowing that he or she has a story that deserves to be heard and that whatever happens, or however busy the day turns out to be, that story will be brought to life around a taped-out stage.

On top of all this, the book will also be about my growth as a storyteller, as I narrate the scenes I witnessed over the past few years when a group of two- to seven-year-olds generously shared their stories with me.

In one of Vivian's letters, she wrote about herself, saying,

Vivian Gussin Paley – Personal Correspondence

I have the easiest task of all. My self-appointed job is simply to tell a good story about the children.

In *The Growth of a Storyteller*, I will take up Vivian's mantra and try my best to tell a good story about the children.

Some of you may have read my previous book, *Princesses, Dragons and Helicopter Stories*, a how-to publication on the Helicopter Stories approach. For others, this might be your first encounter with my work or the Storytelling and Story Acting curriculum of Vivian Gussin Paley. Maybe you have read this introduction and are wondering what it is all about. In that case, I'd better start at the beginning and give you a brief understanding of Vivian Gussin Paley's ethos and how Helicopter Stories works.

The simplest description I can give is that Helicopter Stories involves children telling their stories to an adult scribe, who writes their words verbatim, exactly as they say it. Later the children gather around a taped-out stage and act out all the stories told on that day. In essence, it is an uncomplicated approach, but the child-centred ethos that runs through this and through all of Vivian Gussin Paley's work is what makes it truly remarkable.

But, rather than repeat everything I wrote in *Princesses, Dragons and Helicopter Stories*, which will serve you much better if you are looking for a how-to, I asked some four-, five- and six-year-olds to help me explain Helicopter Stories as if they were talking to a grown-up who had never come across the approach.

Here is their explanation.

(All the children's names have been changed throughout this book to protect anonymity.)

What Are Helicopter Stories?

Alison They're funny.

Daisy You speak stories, and some people write it down.

Isla And you can act it out on the stage.

Ethan So, you think of your own story and tell it to an adult. And the adult writes the story down.

Isla The stories get told. And then you can listen to what character you're going to act out.

Alison They can be scary.

Ethan You're allowed to go and help other people if they are struggling.

Isla Once the story is finished, they get read out, and then the children can decide which character they're going to be. And then that gets circled around, with an underline. And all the other ones just have underlines.

Alison I'm going to be a princess.

Mia We all sit in a big circle, and then we act our stories out.

Isla We sit around the stage. And we don't go past the line. Cause if we go past the line, we need to move back.

Daisy If some people shake their heads like they don't want to come up, they can just be in the last story or the next.

Ethan After that story is finished, we give a clap for those stories.

Alex It's great fun acting them out.

Daisy I like acting.

Isla It's good.

Tamara It's just like you are on a real stage, and you act a story out.

The conversation came to a natural break, so I asked the children where the approach came from and who had invented Storytelling and Story Acting?

The group looked at me with blank faces.

These children know everything there is to know about Helicopter Stories. They are proficient storytellers. For years, they have been telling stories, writing stories and eagerly acting them out. But, none of them had heard of Vivian Gussin Paley.

"She was an author of thirteen publications," I began. "And a kindergarten teacher. She worked with children the same age as you and really cared about their stories." Then, I paused, wanting to tell the group how Vivian was my friend, my mentor for twenty years, how we wrote to each other at least once a month, and I still have every one of her letters. How I went to see her just before she died and held her hand while we said our goodbyes. How she lived until the age of ninety, and how she and her husband Irving loved each other so very much.

But I stopped myself. I had no idea how to put everything I felt for this woman into something as clumsy as words. So I sent a few emails and asked some people I know who love Vivian and her work as much as I do if they would share their thoughts on who she was and the legacy she left behind.

Here are their replies.

Michael Rosen She listened to children.
  She showed us how to listen to children.
Kym Scott Her ability to reflect on her mistakes, to remind herself that she could always try better tomorrow, and most of all, her assertion that all we need to know to best support a child could be learned from the child themselves.
Pie Corbett She respected children and had the insight to listen and watch thoughtfully so she could tell the significant stories of what was happening in her classroom.
Gillian Mcnamee Her room was beyond anything I could imagine. The children were busy becoming good guys and bad guys, princesses, crying babies who needed to go to the doctor, or a puppy getting saved by an eagle. It was a world of imagination.
Nisha Ruparel-Sen She made everyone feel special and had the ability to make deep connections with children and adults alike.
Sarah Sivright Vivian understood the power of stories; children's, adult's, and cultures. She gave them life.
Gail Alder Through reading her thirteen books, I learnt the essence of ethical practice as an Early Years Educator.
Patricia Cooper Vivian was my escort through the forest she discovered in which young children live.
Yu-Ching Huang She was the beacon of my conscience throughout my teaching career.
Nadine Jones She opened the doors of opportunity for me, for the children I have worked with, for those I work with now and for the children I will work with in the future.

Sally Veale Everything about her confirms my belief that children are happiest and learn best when they feel motivated and empowered.

Isla Hill We need not feel alone in leading the learning. The children are always there to ask, to listen to and to follow.

"She sounds nice," said six-year-old Daisy.

"She was," I replied.

1 The Storyteller in Me

"Story is the essential culture builder and learning tool of any society or family or classroom. The child within us and the children in our classes yearn for story."

Vivian Gussin Paley
(Looking for Magpie: Another Voice in the Classroom)

DOI: 10.4324/9781003161400-2

I am a storyteller, a teller of tales.

I find it easier to acknowledge this side of my work than to say I am a writer, even though I do both in equal measures. But "writer" sounds much more serious, as though I know what I am doing. Whereas storyteller sounds like I make it up as I go along.

Which I do.

Mostly.

Don't we all?

When I think about what makes a storyteller, the first image that jumps into my mind is someone who knows many tales. Maybe they grew up surrounded by stories and can weave these elements together, creating new and curious combinations. Storytellers feel like colourful characters, embellishers who convey their meaning through words, images and sounds. I find myself picturing an old woman in a long cloak. It's night-time. She is sitting around a campfire, holding everyone's attention using only the power of her voice.

Being a storyteller suddenly feels like a tall order.

I'm about to scroll up to the top of the page and cross out the sentence where I tell you that I am one, when I stop myself. This is my story. I want to tell you about myself to set the scene for the rest of the book. I will look at how some of the freedom I had as a child growing up in the 1970s varies so greatly from the children I work with today and how it was this independence and access to hours and hours of free, interrupted play that allowed me to develop as a storyteller.

I leave the above sentence unchanged.

The experiences we have and the stories we tell are the things that define us.

A Childhood Rich in Stories

My childhood was rich in stories. I pause again as I write this, wondering if the sentence is true. If there were a lot of stories in my childhood, doesn't that mean there were a lot of books? I think about this and draw a blank. I close my eyes and try to picture a bookcase in my childhood home. From the kitchen to the front room and up the stairs, I travel in my mind, seeing again the peeling purple paint of the bedroom I shared with my sister.

On the wall was a poster of my favourite pop group, the Bay City Rollers. It was covering a large hole. The hole had been created by a magical dragon's egg that had been turned into stone by a curse from an evil witch. I remember my sister making up the story. When she had finished, she threw a very real and very large egg-shaped stone at me so I could see for myself. Unfortunately, I was never any good at Catch. The stone smashed into the wall. If it hadn't have been for that Bay City Rollers poster, I would have been in so much trouble.

My shared bedroom was full of stories, but it did not have a bookcase.

I think deeper, finding it hard to believe there was not one shelf of books, one cabinet of stories, one bookcase of treasures in the place that was my childhood home.

I have spent the last few years ranting about how important stories are in children's lives and how vital it is that they are read to. Yet, when I sit down to think about it, to begin writing a book about the growth of a storyteller, to start sharing the stories I've been told by children over the last few years, I realise that I have no memory of a bookcase in my childhood home.

So I did what any neurotic storyteller would do.

I phoned my mum.

Maybe I couldn't remember. Perhaps there was a bookcase in the hallway or a shelf in the front room. All I needed was my memory prompted, and I would see again those volumes of stories that must have been part of my childhood. For I am a storyteller, and my childhood was surrounded by stories.

"When I was a kid, did we have a bookcase?" I asked, almost as soon as the phone was picked up.

"You what?" said Mum. She had no idea what I was talking about.

"A bookcase or a shelf? Did we have any books?"

My mum paused like it was some kind of trick question and then replied, "Trisha, I was a single parent. We couldn't afford books."

"So, how did you read us our bedtime story?"

I blurted out the question before I had time to compose it more politely. The silence at the end of the phone gave me my answer. There wasn't a bedtime story, nor was there a bookcase. How had I never realised?

A few days later, I was with a group of four- and five-year-olds, and I asked them about the books they owned. These children did not come from an affluent area, and I was keen to see how their situation mirrored my own.

As they answered my questions, I was relieved to hear that all of them owned at least one or two picture books. I know that is not a lot, but I was expecting some of them to have nothing. Research published in 2019 by the National Literacy Trust showed that more than 380,000 UK children aged 9-18 did not own a single book. Perhaps young children are more likely to have books bought for them. Maybe the number of books owned dwindles as children get older. Nowadays, more children's stories are published than when I was a child in the 1970s and getting hold of publications is much easier, but even within this group of children, I could see that poverty was still a barrier. The differences in the quantity and quality of the books these children owned were already apparent.

Gaia I have thousands of stories in my house. They're in my drawer. Last night I was told the bear hunt.

Daisy I got about fifty hundred in my bedroom on a bookshelf.

Alex I got four shelves of books and toys.

Lance I only got a Pokémon book.

Marcus I got Sponge Bob. That's it. I like Sponge Bob.

Next, I asked the children about bedtime stories, hoping that as there were a few more books in their homes than when I was a child, maybe today's four- and five-year-olds were read to more frequently. Again, the responses started well, with several of the children talking about stories as a regular part of their bedtime routine.

Mia My mum tells me stories before bed every night.

Alison I have loads of stories, sometimes my dad comes in and reads them to me, and sometimes my mum, and sometimes I look at the pictures.

Ethan I always have stories at bedtime. Usually, before they read a story, I go and get to have milk and then go to bed, and then Mummy or Daddy reads them to me.

Then it began to change, and the "Sometimes" appeared.

Abby I only sometimes have a story. Not always, but sometimes.

Maddie Sometimes she reads. But sometimes, not all the time.

Bradley Sometimes. I just go straight to bed. When I go to bed early, we have a bath, or a story, sometimes.

And then the "Nevers."

Nadia I brush my teeth and go to bed. I go straight to sleep.

Lawrence I get into my pyjamas, brush my teeth and go to bed. The light gets turned out and the door left open.

Lacey We get a movie, not a story because it's too late.

Of the class of reception-aged children I spoke to, only twenty-five per cent of them regularly had a bedtime story. That's one child in every four. Fifty per cent were read to sometimes, and the remaining twenty-five per cent were never read to at all. One of the replies made me saddest of all. When I asked four-year-old Malcolm whether he ever had a bedtime story, he said, "When I was a little baby, I did. Now I go straight to sleep." The notion that at four years old, you have grown too big to be read a story is heart-breaking. But Malcolm is not alone. In the USA, in 2018, children's book publisher Scholastic surveyed parents of children aged from birth to five years old about the number of times they read to their child. The results showed that only fifty-five per cent of under fives were read to at least five days a week, and only thirty-seven per cent were read to daily. Scholastic's research found that as children grow older, they are more likely to become a frequent reader if they are read to aloud between five and seven days a week before starting nursery. According to their survey, forty-five per cent of children do not have this opportunity.

These findings echo the results gathered in 2017 by Gillian Washington, a UK primary school teacher based in West Yorkshire. She decided to find out how many children in her school regularly heard a bedtime story. The answer was less than a third. This drove her to start a local campaign, which she called Bring Back the Bedtime Story. South Parade Primary School in Ossett, Wakefield launched the programme with a parents evening explaining the immense value of stories, not only educationally, but also for creating precious family moments. While their parents were at the launch, the children lay on blankets in their classroom and had a story and a hot chocolate in their pyjamas. They even created a chant, "What do we want, bedtime stories. When do we want them NOW." The work paid off, and the feedback was tremendous.

But what about the children who don't have access to this campaign?

In some ways, the lack of being read to and the limited access to books in the homes of many of the children I work with is similar to my own experiences of childhood. But does the fact that children are not being read to in the twenty-first century have a more significant impact on these children than it did on me when I was a child?

I began to think about the other areas of my childhood that influenced my growth as a storyteller.

Stories in the Streets

The great outdoors was where most of my adventures happened. That was the stage where our stories were acted out. We'd play for hours in the woods near my house, or running up and down the street, pretending to be characters from the television, or ones we had made up. I remember spending whole days with my sister and the other children in our street just playing outside. We created a gang called The Dirt Collectors, who solved mysteries and were always looking for clues. Our name came from a soap powder advert that cheerfully asked, "Is your son a dirt collector?" The fact that we were a group of female Dirt Collectors felt strangely empowering.

I remember one time when my sister and I outlined a giant footprint in a pile of sand left by some builders. Then she tied me to a lamppost with a skipping rope. She left me for hours, but I didn't mind. I spent all that time pretending to be Ann Darrow and acting out the terror of being sacrificed to King Kong. I shared my woes with anyone who happened to be passing but refused to let them untie me. It was only when I didn't turn up for dinner that my sister remembered me. When she came to untie me there was panic in her eyes, but I'd had a great afternoon, performing my one-woman show to anyone who would listen.

Sadly, everything I have just shared about the stories of the street are experiences that many children in the UK today will never have. The culture of playing outside, of spending whole days wandering pavements, or parks, unaccompanied by adults, sometimes bored, sometimes so lost in a story that you forget about time, relies on a belief that the streets are safe.

Research by the UK National Children's Bureau in 2012 showed that nearly fifty per cent of parents have a fear of strangers that prevents them from allowing their children to play outside. It's not that there is a rise in crime. There is nothing to show that there are more child kidnappings these days, but it seems like our fears as parents are based on a sense that this is the case. Nowadays, the news is on twenty-four hours a day, so when anything does happen, we hear about it quicker and often for longer. This can create a false sense of the level of danger that exists for our children. Also, there is a lot more traffic on the roads. Playing on the streets today means learning to navigate between rows of parked cars. Add to this, that as a society, we are becoming risk-averse. This is stopping our children from having the experiences we had when we were their age. My story of being tied to a lamppost and left for a couple of hours, an experience that still makes me smile, would never be allowed to happen today. Neither would the hours of time we spent away from an adult, with only what existed on the streets to entertain us.

In 2018, a National Trust survey found that children spend less than half the time playing outside than their parents did when they were children. A study in the same year by the UK Government found that ten per cent of parents had not taken their children to a park, a forest, or a beach for at least a year. For too many children, the opportunities to engage with outside spaces, particularly on their own, is much lower than it ever used to be.

When I was a child, the freedom I had to wander the streets and the woods gave me the space to develop my stories. But where is this freedom for our children now? If they are not read to at home, and they don't have any time alone outside, then that space to make up their own stories, to exercise their own imagination, is much harder to come by.

Vivian Gussin Paley – Personal Correspondence

Something else has become clear to me, as your work suggests. Play and story-telling must be practiced.

The children you have worked with for several years continue to expand their narrative and acting skills. Somehow we must convince teachers and parents that these are skills we are teaching.

Many teachers I meet do not really believe that play is a subject with skills to be observed, practiced, developed, and mastered. Sometimes I think the best aspect to storytelling and acting is that it creates more respect for play itself.

Borrowed Stories

It was then that I remembered how important the library was to me. How borrowed copies of Enid Blyton's *Faraway Tree* books filled my childhood with Dame Washalot, Moon-Face and Silky the Fairy. When the lights went out at night, my sister and I would lie opposite each other in single beds, and in hushed voices, we would make up adventures about the top of the Faraway Tree and the lands that we'd find there.

There were no bookcases in my childhood home, but we didn't need one. Books didn't stay at our house very long. They lay on the carpet by my bed for the shortest of times. Then, when they were finished, they were gone, replaced by the next borrowed story.

Read and Return.

I have no memory of whether I borrowed the same books more than once or if some stories just stayed with me longer, but I can still taste the magic of the Faraway Tree, and when I shut my eyes, I can imagine that I am back there.

When I look at my bookcase now, it is full of dusty stories, some of which I have not yet got around to reading. As a child, knowing my time with a book was finite would always spur me to finish it. Suddenly, I crave the urgency of Read and Return, of having an end date where stories are taken from me, so I'm forced to finish the ones I've started.

But libraries are closing.

Since 2010, almost eight hundred libraries have closed in the UK, and thousands of children have not been able to experience the thrill of choosing any book on the shelf. My library card gave me access to hundreds of stories, bookcases full of them. Yet in the UK today, many children growing up in poverty, who do not have a bookcase in their home or a parent who can afford to buy books like in my household, no longer have the same on-tap access to stories that I had as a child; a sad indictment of the sixth richest country in the world.

Thankfully, organisations like the Book Trust are working to change this, distributing 3.3 million books to families every year, getting stories to babies in the first year of their life, and providing publications in thirty-five different languages. But for real change to happen, governments need to open their eyes to the importance of reading and making up stories as a gateway to enhancing children's life chances. How can our children ever hope to fully develop in their growth as storytellers if these essential ingredients are denied them?

As the world changes, we must change with it to ensure we remain relevant and are equipped to meet the needs of children now and in the future. There's never been a more urgent time for us to focus our efforts, redefine our approach, and set out how we will inspire and encourage a new generation of children on their reading journeys.

(The Next Chapter – Book Trust 2021 Strategy)

Not only do children from disadvantaged backgrounds have considerably lower school attainment and lower adult earnings than their peers from more affluent backgrounds, we also find large differences in the outcomes of children from disadvantaged backgrounds across the country.

(Laura van der Erve, Senior Research Economist, Institute for Fiscal Studies, 2020)

Vivian Gussin Paley – Personal Correspondence

The climate for the soft arts is cloudy and threatening these days. Though I keep receiving invitations to speak about fantasy play and stories, the talk is all about the new standards and testing. Even the threes and fours are being bombarded with questions that have nothing to do with who they are and what they know.

One such question, on a new test with which to judge 4 year olds, reads the word Card. Now point to the picture of what it will become if I take away the D. The child is supposed to point to a car in a row of pictures.

How can anyone possibly think that this is a nicer thing to do to a child than to sit and do stories with them?

The Most Unlikely of Routes

As I think about all the aspects that have fed my growth as a storyteller, I remember another part of my story. It was not just the library books that fed my imagination, nor was it only the stories that we made up on the street. I was also lucky enough to have the theatre, an unusual benefit for a working-class girl growing up in the 1970s. This gift came to me through the most unlikely of routes.

My mum was a Dr Barnardo's child born in Ireland in 1934. Orphaned from birth, she was shipped over to England and brought up in the Essex Girls Home. My childhood experience of theatre was bequeathed me by a chance set of events in my mother's life.

In April 1942, a woman called Alex, who was unable to have children of her own, visited the Essex Girls Home to see if she could mentor one of the girls. My eight-year-old mum was selected. Alex was allowed to visit every couple of weeks and take my mum on trips. They went to the theatre, the ballet, art galleries, the law courts, and even walked around the dome of St Paul's Cathedral. Alex showed my mum a London she had never seen before, and the experience widened her world. The privilege of attending high-quality live performances and being taken to some of the most prestigious places in London was unheard of for an orphan from that time, but thanks to Alex's kindness over many years, my mum developed a lifelong love of theatre that she passed on to me.

Although my mum was a single parent and money was scarce, two or three times a year, as birthday treats for both myself and my sister, she always found a way to buy three tickets, high up in the gods, at the Bristol Hippodrome. There we would watch a show, often through a shared pair of theatre binoculars that cost five pence to release from the seat in front. My love of theatre was born.

Going to the theatre two or three times a year influenced the storyteller I became. Then I remember the legacy that has been left for our newest generation of storytellers, and I feel incredibly sad. Theatre in Education was a key part of my primary education, with a theatre company coming into my school once a year. I remember aged nine realising that acting was a job, and when the actors came to our classroom to talk about the show, it was all I wanted to know about. With cuts in arts funding, Theatre in Education happens much less, and if children don't experience theatre, they may never get to realise that the arts are a job that is open to them.

But this is not the only disadvantage our Early Years children of today have inherited. Growing up in the twenty-first century, these children inhabit a world where our education systems increasingly value knowledge over creativity. Nowadays, a formal approach to learning is being pushed onto younger and younger children, children who are having the time set aside to play, to imagine, to be, squeezed and reduced in every corner of their lives.

On an episode of Question Time in 2013, Michael Gove, the then UK Secretary of State for Education, said,

> Creativity depends on mastering certain skills and acquiring a body of knowledge before being able to give expression to what's in you… You cannot be creative unless you understand how sentences are constructed, what words mean and how to use grammar.
>
> (Michael Gove, 26 February 2013)

When I listen to a four-year-old telling their story to an adult scribe or seen a three-year-old's face light up as they say the words, "Dinosaur, Raah," I know in my heart that this attitude is not true. It is written in the expression on their faces, and I just know that there's a bigger story bubbling away inside.

When I hear this outdated argument that the acquisition of knowledge should come before creativity I find myself thinking of Mr Gradgrind in the opening lines of Charles Dickens novel *Hard Times*.

> Now, what I want is facts. Teach these boys and girls nothing but facts. Facts alone are wanted in life. Plant nothing else, and root out everything else. You can only form the mind of a reasoning animal upon Facts: nothing else will ever be of any service to them.

The difference between the two is that Gradgrind was a parody and eventually saw the error of his ways, whereas sadly, the damage of this ideology is being felt in many schools today.

The more I look at the circumstances our young children are growing up in, the more I realise how high the odds are stacked against them, and yet, somehow, against all probability, they are still highly skilful storytellers.

But how is that possible?

In his book *From Two to Five*, Russian children's poet Kornei Chukovsky tells of a diary kept by E. I. Stanchinskaia, a scientist and mother, who wrote about the first seven years of her son's life. Raising a child in Moscow in the 1920s, Stanchinskaia subscribed to the common dogma of the time that fantasy was dangerous. She did everything in her power to "protect" her son from fairy tales. For the first seven years of his life, Stanchinskaia's son was only exposed to realistic stories. However, "... her boy, as if to make up for the fairy tales of which he had been deprived, began to spin from morning till night the wildest fantasies." (Chukovsky, 1933, p. 119).

The boy pretended that a red elephant came to live in his room; he invented an imaginary friend. When it snowed, he pretended to be a reindeer, and holding out his empty hands, told his mum he was giving her a baby tiger. Stanchinskaia's son behaved like any imaginative child, and despite the fact that he never heard any fantasy stories, the diary reveals that he created his own fantasy world.

In her article, "Looking for Magpie, Another Voice in the Classroom," Vivian Gussin Paley said,

> Children enter school accomplished storytellers, veteran fantasy players, only to discover quite abruptly that this great passion of theirs is not part of the curriculum. Their talent for imagery and illusion are sent outdoors to play, where no teacher can make use of the stories they tell – or even hear them.
>
> (Paley, 1995, p. 95)

The last time I saw Vivian, she asked me, "With all the changes that are happening in the world, with all the advances in technology, have things got any better for the children?" It was a difficult question to answer, and it summed up the importance Vivian still placed on making the world a better place for the youngest among us, even though she knew she was dying. But what could I say? Almost one-third of children in the UK are living in poverty, and less than fifty per cent of under-fives ever hear a bedtime story. The streets are perceived as unsafe, and the time given for fantasy play is growing shorter and shorter.

However, there was a positive, one that I could share and that I believe with all my heart. So I told Vivian, there are still hundreds and thousands of us who work in the Early Years, who trust in the value of play. Vivian's work and the work of others like her give us the power to fight for what we know is right. I believe that things do change for the better for children who regularly have access to Helicopter Stories, and there are many people across the world who agree with me.

Vivian Gussin Paley's approach means children are listened to, and even in the challenging times through which we live, they are still creating and discovering, making up plot and dialogue and daring to reinvent mythology against all the odds.

We have a hard job to do. Many of the children entering our settings and schools have had less access to stories, to time alone, to books and make-believe than I had as a child. However, as Vivian Gussin Paley said, they are still arriving in our settings and schools as storytellers. If we can provide them with a rich story environment, where they regularly hear stories and poems, where they are listened to and frequently have their stories scribed and acted out around a taped-out stage, then it is my belief that these innate storytelling skills will flourish, and they will grow as storytellers.

INTRODUCING THE FIRST TROUPE OF STORYTELLERS

From Birth to Two

**Actors, writers, storytellers, directors
who took part in the longitudinal study
(in alphabetical order)**

Aiysha, Anthony, Charlotte, Jasper,
Muhammad, Ollie, Peter, Sergio, Sofia

2 The Truly Youngest Storytellers

"They do not pretend to be storytellers; they are storytellers. It is their intuitive approach to all occasions. It is the way they think."

Vivian Gussin Paley
(*The Boy Who Would Be a Helicopter*)

DOI: 10.4324/9781003161400-3

What are storytellers made of?
What are storytellers made of?
They have questions galore,
And an imagination that soars.
That's what storytellers are made of.

What are storytellers made of?
What are storytellers made of?
They are me and you,
It is what we all do.
That's what storytellers are made of.

In the thirty seconds or so that it took you to read from the top of this page to the word you are staring at *now*, there were approximately one hundred and twenty-five babies born across the world. That is one hundred and twenty-five creative individuals taking their first breath on the journey that is their life. Each has already inhaled their earliest taste of a world that thrives on stories, a world where they will develop as storytellers.

Imagine all the things that will happen to these boys and girls along the way, the places they will go, the things they will see, the adventures they will have – so many possibilities. Today is the start of their story, a story that began a long time ago, with their parents, their grandparents, their grandparent's parents. Now it is their turn to stand on the stage and become the main character – the hero.

Starring as the protagonist of their own story, our heroes will face hardships along the way. They will meet people who are unkind and do mean things that make them sad. There will be scary moments filled with unexpected change and times when they are forced to make difficult choices that will affect their lives. But, there will be extraordinary times too. Times when they cannot believe how wonderful the world is, when their faces ache from smiling, and they wake up believing anything is possible. In these times, they will feel like a hero at the start of a journey.

The Hero's Journey

In his book, *The Hero With A Thousand Faces*, Joseph Campbell outlines the concept of the Hero's Journey, the most frequently used story structure in existence, shared by cultures worldwide and followed by most narratives. The Hero's Journey is present in stories that are as far removed in time as the Ancient Greek Myth of *Theseus and the Minotaur* is from *Harry Potter and the Philosopher's Stone*. Amazingly, this structure is also present in stories told by children at the start of their growth as storytellers, even though they have no prior knowledge of it.

The Hero's Journey contains twelve steps that a hero must take to achieve his or her purpose. Stories do not need to cover every stage of the hero's journey, and sometimes the order is muddled around, but once you understand this universal structure, it is hard not to notice aspects of it in all the stories you encounter. That scene when the hero nearly dies but comes back to life at the last moment – that is the Resurrection. Or when the hero refuses to go on an adventure that you know they have to go on, or there will be no story – that is the Refusal of the Call. These ingredients may sound formulaic, but they work because they present us with a familiar pattern that is deeply satisfying.

The Twelve Stages of the Hero's Journey

1. **Ordinary World**
   We meet the hero at the start of the story in their ordinary everyday environment. Harry Potter is in the cupboard under the stairs at the Dursley's, Little Red Riding Hood is at home with her mother.

2. **Call to Adventure**
   Something happens to change the path for our hero. For Harry, it is the invitation to go to Hogwarts. For Little Red Riding Hood it's her mother asking her to take a basket of goodies to grandma.

3. **Refusal of the Call**
   The refusal of the call reminds us of the dangers that lie ahead. Sometimes this can be a complete refusal to take the next step, and other times it is a brief moment where we are reminded that the path won't be easy. Red Riding Hood seems willing to begin her journey, but her mother reminds her of the dangers of straying from the path, and although Harry follows Hagrid willingly, we know that he is riddled with self-doubt.

4. **Meeting the Mentor**
   Alongside every hero is the mentor who supports them. For Red Riding Hood, it's her mother, reminding her that the world is a dangerous place. For Harry, it is Hagrid introducing him to the wizarding world.

5. **Crossing the Threshold**
   Crossing the threshold can be a physical act. Red Riding Hood walks into the forest. Harry walks through the wall onto platform 9¾ – But crossing the threshold can also be an awakening. Harry's destiny changes when he discovers that Voldemort killed his parents. He crosses the threshold into a world that looks very different from how it did before. From then onwards, his life will never be the same.

6. Tests, Allies and Enemies

Once the hero has crossed the threshold, they are confronted with situations that test them. There are friends and enemies along the route who are there to help or hinder them. On the train to Hogwarts, Harry meets Ron and Hermione, as well as his enemy Draco Malfoy. Red Riding Hood talks to the wolf, and later in the story, she is helped by the woodcutter. This is also the time for tests. For Harry, he needs to learn new magical skills, whereas Red Riding Hood is tested on her ability to stick to the rules and not talk to strangers.

7. Approach to the Inmost Cave

As the hero approaches the inmost cave they are nearing the heart of their journey. This is the ticking clock, time is running out, and the stakes are heightened. What our hero does now will affect the course of their journey. A troll is loose in Hogwarts, someone is trying to steal the philosopher's stone, and Red Riding Hood has stepped off the path to pick flowers.

8. The Ordeal

Everything our hero has been doing up until now is building towards this moment. This is life and death, where the hero faces their fears. Harry and his friends need to overcome the obstacles that have been set up to protect the Philosophers Stone. Red Riding Hood is confronted with the wolf dressed as Grandma but she doesn't recognise him.

9. Reward

Here we take a breather from the danger, and it seems that all of the struggles were worth it. Harry sees the Philosopher's Stone being placed into his pocket. Red Riding Hood recognises something is wrong with grandma's ears, eyes and mouth, But for both of them it's too late. Voldemort knows where the stone is, and Red Riding Hood is swallowed whole. For a brief moment it looked as if everything was okay, but it wasn't.

10. The Road Back

Something needs to happen to push the hero back into their ordinary world. This is the turning point. Harry faces Voldemort, who is attached to the back of Professor Quirrell's head. The Huntsman rushes into Grandma's cottage. This moment pushes the hero to action, heightening the stakes.

11. Resurrection

In many stories, there is a meeting with death, the final part of the journey before the hero can return to the ordinary world. Once they do, they are reborn wiser from the lessons of their journey. Harry wakes in the hospital and discovers that he is protected by his mother's love. Red Riding Hood and grandma are pulled out of the wolf's belly, alive and safe, finally understanding the dangers of the woods.

12. Return with the Elixir

Then they return to home, changed from their experience. Harry returns to Privet Drive, happy to know that he is part of Hogwarts. Red Riding Hood returns home safe, braver and more aware of the dangers that exist in the world outside.

Campbell's Hero's Journey is recognised by storytellers, novelists, scriptwriters and film producers globally and it is widely accepted that the majority of stories follow the same basic pattern. The hero is pushed into an adventure – he or she faces difficulties – fights with enemies – and returns home changed from the experience. That, in a nutshell, is what we call story, and as human beings, we can't get enough of it. Our brains are hardwired to make sense of the world through story form so much so, that even the stories our young children tell are already beginning to contain elements of this structure.

> For over 150,000 years, before there was writing, human beings relied on story as a structure and storytelling as a process to communicate essential history, values, attitudes, beliefs. Because we relied on story to communicate and to archive in human memory, because there was no writing, what it has literally done is evolutionarily rewire the human brain so that humans were born to make sense of the world in story terms.
>
> (Kendal Haven on YouTube – MediaX Seminar Your Brain on Story, 2015)

During his MediaX Seminar, *Your Brain On Story*, Kendal Haven told the audience that this belief that we are wired for story was first proposed by evolutionary biologists and then tested extensively by developmental psychologists. It is now widely accepted as fact. We are storytelling animals. We think in story. We dream in story. We understand everything that is happening around us through story. With story ingrained in everything we do, it is hardly surprising that the children I scribe for, regardless of their age, take to storytelling so effortlessly.

Tamara – age 5

Once upon a time, there lived a little girl. And once, she went to the forest. And she saw a wolf. And he was a bad wolf. He was chasing her around the forest. The wolf got her. But she got out of his hands, and she went to find her mummy. She went home and closed the door. And she was safe.

Tamara's story fits the model of The Hero's Journey. The little girl is the hero. She goes into the forest, a symbolic story location filled with mystery and danger. Then she meets a wolf (the baddie). The girl is caught. This is the climax of the story, the moment of danger. Luckily she manages to escape. The girl searches for Mummy and eventually goes home and closes the door. At the end of the story, she's safe.

The Hero's Journey is a universal story structure that connects with us at a deeply psychological level. This is why elements of it are present in so many stories dictated by children, even though they are just beginning their growth as storytellers. The structure of the Hero's Journey taps into our desire to become a better version of ourselves. It is a version where we can overcome obstacles and battle monsters to become stronger, wiser and braver. Tamara, at age five, protected herself from the wolf by escaping. At that moment, she was powerful.

Meeting the Mentor

In Joseph Campbell's outline of the hero's journey, the hero meets a mentor and is presented with a gift. This could be training, advice, or a magical talisman that will help them overcome the difficulties they will face. When we care for children, we become their mentors. What better gifts can we give to our heroes born today than the gift of stories.

Stories contain magic. They enable us to climb outside of our everyday lives and see what the world looks like further afield. They give us a view of the world beyond our experiences. It is as if we are standing on the topmost branch of the tallest tree and can see for miles around. In stories, anything is possible. We can fly on magic carpets, visit imaginary worlds, or sail across the ocean. We can escape from danger, or battle a troll, or stand up to a bully. In stories, heroes build resilience to conquer the challenges thrown at them.

In her book *Proust and the Squid: The Story and Science of the Reading Brain*, Maryanne Wolf says that when we read a story, we leave our own consciousness and "pass over" into the experiences of the person we are reading about.

> When we "pass over" into how a knight thinks, how a slave feels, how a heroine behaves, and how an evildoer can regret or deny wrongdoing, we never come back quite the same.
>
> (Wolf, 2008, p. 8.)

This is why it is vital we enhance the story diet of every child we know. It is never too early to begin the process of sharing a story with those babies born today. By surrounding children in a language-rich environment, where they're read to often, told stories regularly and have the chance to make up stories of their own, we prepare them for the road ahead. This is why at MakeBelieve Arts we created an audio only programme of stories entitled The Story Basket, to accompany Helicopter Stories. It is essential that children have the opportunity to listen to high-quality stories and be taken on a journey of their imagination.

Maryanne Wolf says that when we hold babies in our arms and read them a story, we build an association in their mind, that the act of being read to is linked to a sensation of being loved. I found these words incredibly moving. Whether it's a tale from a book or one that is made up, what better feeling is there than being held in someone's arms and listening to the rhythmic, sing-song voice of a story being told.

But the benefits don't end there. For babies, the words they hear, the pictures they see and the expressions they witness on the storyteller's face all build towards a growing understanding of language and meaning. As our heroes begin to notice the marks on the page, they gradually realise that marks make words, and words make stories. Of course, the best thing about stories is that they can be read again and again and again. The same is true when a child engages in Helicopter Stories. During the scribing process, they see their words becoming marks on the page, making the connection between the spoken and the written word. Later, when their story is acted out, their words, the characters they have imagined are brought to life in 3D.

> Children who never have a story read to them, who never hear words that rhyme, who never imagine fighting with dragons or marrying a prince, have the odds overwhelmingly against them.
>
> (Wolf, 2008, p. 20)

This gift of story that we give to our heroes born today suddenly feels more meaningful. Did you know that the number of times a child is read to or fails to be read to during the first five years of their life is one of the most significant predictors of their later reading and language skills? Let's hope these newborn heroes engage with thousands of stories throughout their lifetime.

A weird thought jumps into my mind. Some of the stories that our heroes born today will grow to love and share with their own children have not even been dreamed up yet by the person who will eventually tell them. That is the beautiful thing about stories. They keep being told and retold, and new ones invented. Our thirst for stories is unquenchable.

Vivian Gussin Paley wrote to me once about a three-year-old girl, Rebecca, who told her the story, "Once Upon a Time!" Vivian asked Rebecca how she would act this story out. Rebecca got up and skipped around the table.

"Like that," she said.

Vivian remarked that this simple solution demonstrated the passage of time quite brilliantly. Later, when the story was acted out, the other storytellers were so impressed that, for a while, all their stories began that way.

This fascination with the beginnings of stories was echoed in a classroom I was working with when Benji developed the habit of starting his stories by saying the word "once" nine times.

Once, once, once, once, once, once, once, once, once.

He had been doing this for a while when one day he said to me, "I still want my stories to have a lot of once, but then I don't have room for the rest." He pointed at the page where the word "once" was written nine times. It took up more than half the available space.

"How about, if the next time you tell a story, I write the word 'once', only one time," I said. "Then I'll put in brackets the number of times you want me to say it. That way, it won't take up so much room." Benji was happy with this, and for several months all his stories started,

Once (x9)

The importance both these children placed on this opening phrase demonstrates the magic contained in those words. When the storyteller says "Once…" we are instantly drawn in. The story is about to start. We take our place around the fire, eager to know what will happen next.

Tests, Allies and Enemies

In the world of our heroes, there will be the goodies who he or she will grow to love. But there will also be the baddies: the mean ones, those who are unkind or make the hero scared. A vital aspect of the Hero's Journey is for the hero to learn how to overcome these dangers. My older storytellers, the four- and five-year-olds, know all about the baddies. Whether it's phoning their parents to rescue them when they are trapped by a dragon or escaping from a wolf in the forest, they have plenty of ideas on how to deal with baddies.

> ### Gaia – age 5
>
> Once upon a time, there was a dragon. Then he found some people. Then he started to chase them. And he put them in a cage. But one of the friends had a phone, and quietly she called her mum and dad. They came to rescue them, and they brought them home.

The people in the cage were able to escape the dragon. By imagining a mobile phone, five-year-old Gaia effortlessly created a solution to rescue them. At four and five, children easily recognise baddies in stories and find ways for the goodies to break free. But when does this ability start? Can newborn babies recognise baddies? Surely goodies and baddies are not something babies are aware of until they are much older? Then I came across the research of Developmental Psychologist Paul Bloom from Yale University.

Bloom was investigating kindness when he asked the question, "Are we born nice?" At the time, many people, scientists included, believed that the answer to this question was no. They thought we had no inherent kindness within us and felt that it was something we learned from our environment. Paul Bloom's team decided to study this further. They created two animated films that they showed to babies aged six months and ten months.

In the first animation, a dome-shaped creature is trying to get up a steep hill. Every time the creature gets close to the top, he slips back down to the bottom. After a few goes at this, a square-shaped creature appears and helps to push the dome until it successfully reaches the top of the hill.

In the second animation, the dome-shaped creature is back and again tries to reach the top of the hill. This time a triangle-shaped creature appears, and rather than helping, it pushes the dome back to the bottom of the hill. At the end of this animation, the triangle-shaped creature and the square-shaped creature appear at the top of the screen. The dome walks over and stands next to the square. After staying there for a while, he walks over to the triangle and stands next to it.

Even as you read this, your brain is probably giving these shapes personalities. You have cast the dome as the hero. Our hero has a goal, to reach the top of the hill. You have seen the square as an ally, helping our hero to get there. The triangle is the baddy, holding our hero back. But this analogy seems really sophisticated. At six or ten months old, can babies really think like that?

Before this experiment was carried out, it had already been established that babies will look longer at things that surprise them than they will at things that seem ordinary. This makes sense; it is the things outside of the ordinary that we are most curious about, that most hold our attention. Using this knowledge, Paul Bloom's team recorded where the babies' eyes rested the longest. They discovered, overwhelmingly, that babies at both six and ten months looked longer when the dome was standing next to the mean triangle. It was as if they were surprised that the dome would choose to stand next to the triangle after the triangle had been so cruel.

Wondering if the babies were being influenced by the shapes or colours they had used, Paul Bloom's team ran the experiment repeatedly, swapping colours and using the square as the baddy and the triangle as the goodie. Each time, the babies registered surprise when the protagonist stood by the shape that had stopped it from getting up the hill.

Paul Bloom's team tested this further. They created a puppet show, where a tiger was happily playing with a ball. The tiger dropped the ball, and a rabbit picked it up. The tiger and the rabbit looked at each other as if working out what to do. Then the rabbit rolled the ball back to the tiger. The tiger continued to play. Then he dropped the ball again. A different rabbit picked it up. The tiger and the second rabbit looked at each other as if working out what to do. Suddenly, the second rabbit ran off, taking the ball with him. The tiger was left on its own, and the puppet show ended.

After the show, both rabbits were offered to the baby to choose from. Overwhelmingly, the babies reached for the goodie, the one who had given the tiger back his ball. They hugged that puppet tightly. Wondering at what age this preference would kick in, the team tried the experiment with a group of three-month-old babies. Although babies at this age cannot reach, they can demonstrate their preference by where they look. The team knew from the previous studies that the babies would tend to look at the puppet they wanted to hug, so they held up both characters and noted which one the three-month-olds looked at. It was always the goodie.

These experiments have been interpreted by the authors of this study to show that babies have an innate ability to care for others. They suggest that from birth, humans have the capacity to make moral judgements. That we have an inbuilt sense of fair and unfair. This links with storytelling. When babies identify with the good rabbit or the kind square, they demonstrate the same kind of empathy that we feel for the characters in our stories.

The question, "which character do I want to be like?" is a fundamental component of how we lose ourselves in a story. We need to relate to the hero. We want to be like them as this makes us feel connected. If I watch someone drop their ball, I want to be the one who picks it up and returns it, not the mean one who grabs it and runs away. Paul Bloom's research demonstrates that this potential for understanding the world through story form is present in babies, even before they can reach, or stand or crawl, and this will only get stronger as our heroes grow older.

As we read to our babies, or make up stories with them, or share rhymes, they begin to discover the wonderful sounds they can make with their mouths, loud and soft, gurgled and cooed, giggled and chuckled. Before we know it, a baby's burbles and babbles will turn into words, words will turn into phrases and phrases into stories of their own.

Language in the Crib

In the late 1950s, a linguist named Ruth Hirsch Weir decided to study her twenty-one-month-old son Anthony's pre-sleep monologues. Most toddlers will engage in this type of pre-sleep chatter, burbling to themselves until they eventually fall asleep. However, Ruth is one of the few parents who has taken time to study this in-depth. By tape recording and transcribing Anthony's words and sounds as he lay in his cot, Ruth discovered a linguistical sense to his mutterings.

In her book *Language in the Crib*, Ruth discusses how certain words and phrases that Anthony used repeatedly appeared across many of her recordings. Sometimes the tone of her son's voice or the inflections he used imitated adult speech even if what he was saying was unintelligible. Ruth also noticed that where her son spoke words that were made up or did not make sense, she could pick up patterns of sounds or examples of where these rhymed. Anthony also seemed to be playing with rhythm and alliteration, creating what Ruth Weir describes as a "strange kind of poetry."

Here is one of Anthony's creations.

Like a piggy bank.
Like a piggy bank.
Had a pink sheet on.
The grey pig out.
(Weir, 1962, p. 104)

So many Ps and Bs, I can taste its tango on my tongue. But I also couldn't help thinking about it from a different perspective. Reading Ruth Weir's book, I found myself reflecting on the link between Anthony's pre-sleep monologues and the stories I am told by the two- and-three-year-olds I work with. I imagined myself leading the acting out of the pig poem above, inviting Anthony and some other children to pretend to put money in a piggy bank, to wrap themselves up in pink sheets and to totter around the stage like the grey pig. Clues gathered from the acting out might have led me to believe that the pig had escaped, or perhaps it had just climbed out of its pigsty for an early morning walk. I might never have discovered the true meaning behind the story. Still, I would have come away with a sense of Anthony's thinking from the activity of placing this story on the stage.

In one of Ruth Weir's recordings, Anthony repeated the phrase "Daddy dance," again and again. It is as if an image of his daddy dancing had caught his imagination and become part of the words and imagery he played with as he lay in his cot. Ruth makes a point of telling her reader that Anthony's daddy rarely danced, which makes it even more curious as to why this twenty-one-month-old was so fixated on repeating this phrase. Perhaps, as Ruth Weir suggests, it was the alliteration of the words that he enjoyed, or maybe it was a memory of seeing daddy dancing and wishing that it would happen again. If only I could see how Anthony would move if this two-word story was acted out. This might give some clues to the meaning. Maybe Daddy jiggled up and down as he rocked Anthony to sleep, and in the acting out, this would become apparent. Or perhaps Daddy was dancing absentmindedly once, and Anthony saw him. We shall never know.

Vivian Gussin Paley – Personal Correspondence

You picked up on an important part of the deal, every story phrase or word, must be acted out. It matters not a bit if the process goes fast, leaving out the extra stage business. What must not ever be left out is a child's story, even if it has to be done on the way to the bus.

In his book, *Entranced By Story*, Hugo Crago, a psychoanalyst, wonders whether the repetition of "Daddy Dance" is linked to Anthony's anxiety that daddy doesn't dance anymore. Maybe Anthony believes that this is something he is responsible for. Whatever the reason, Crago believes that the phrase is essential because Anthony repeats it so often.

> It shouldn't surprise us that the earliest "art form" that a toddler composes might take the form of patterned sound, for experts theorise that before human beings spoke, they "sang"... Nor should it surprise us that a toddler's compositions might express feelings... "Daddy Dance" returns several times: that is the clue that alerts us to the possible meaning of Anthony's "song."
>
> (Crago, 2016, p. 17)

Hugo Crago calls these compositions "songs," whereas I call them stories. Either way, we both agree that for Anthony, they held meaning. Having scribed for children aged twenty months and above, I know that the words and sounds captured on Ruth Weir's tape recorder would not be out of place alongside the wordplay and poetry I've scribed and that have been acted out by the toddlers and two-year-olds I have worked with.

I remember a story told to me by a two-year-old named Muhammad.

Muhammad – age 2

Me, Me, Me, Me, Me, Me, Me.
Me, Me, Me, Me, Me, Me, Me.
Me, Me, Me, Me, Me, Me, Me.

Each time Muhammad dictated a row of "Me's" for me to write down, he did so in a staccato voice, keeping the rhythm exactly the same. I repeated the "Me's" back to him as I wrote each word down. This made him smile, enjoying the sound of his story being mirrored back. As we acted out Muhammad's story, all of the two-year-olds jumped up and down, and up and down, and up and down, saying "Me, Me, Me, Me, Me, Me, Me" with joyful abandon.

Some people might wonder if the word "Me" can be a story? I think it can. It has the first ingredients of one – a lead character. Children's early stories introduce us to the hero. Whether that hero is me, me, me, or a fish, or a mummy, or a person driving a car, they have taken the first step on the hero's journey and presented us with the hero.

Cause and Effect – A Different Type of Story

Early story play can also be seen in a toddler exploring the cause-and-effect relationship between two objects.

Imagine a young child playing with a truck and a dinosaur.
Maybe she is repeatedly smashing the two objects together.   BANG
Watching as the dinosaur knocks into the truck.   BANG
Then pulling them apart again, until,   BANG

They collide with each other once more.

This seemingly random act of cause and effect contains the essence of story – two disconnected pieces coming together.   BANG

And something happens.

This, in its most basic form, is the structure of a story. The hero's journey.

Take a boy who is forced to live under the stairs and an evil wizard.
Bring them together and,   BANG
Something happens.

Take a girl who can move objects with her mind and an incredibly nasty headteacher.
Bring them together and,   BANG
Something happens.

Cause and effect is a vital part of story creation. Narratives consist of a chain of cause-and-effect relationships – *this happens. As a result, this happens, and as a result, this happens.* Our ability to understand story and create stories of our own relies on our capacity to understand cause and effect. Exploring cause and effect is the beginning of story play for our youngest storytellers. Even with the story of "Me, me, me, me, me," this play is evident. I am the character in this story. Me. Me. Me. Me. Me. What would happen if the story was just me? Will she write down my words?

In Mrs Tully's Room

As our toddlers grow, they continue their exploration of cause and effect. Combine this with their drive to communicate and their curiosity that knows no bounds, and you find yourself in the company of the anarchists of the story world – the two-year-olds.

In the fifth year of her retirement, Vivian Gussin Paley was approached by a kindergarten teacher, Lillian Tully, who asked, "Would you care to see the truly youngest storytellers? The Twos?"

Taking up the invitation, Vivian found herself in a room filled with the youngest of storytellers. She describes her first impressions of this age group in her book *In Mrs Tully's Room*.

> They seem to own everything they touch. "Mine!" they announce and then move on. It is a dolls corner in motion, and the children themselves are the dolls, carrying supplies in buggies and baskets to every other corner of the room.
>
> (Paley, 2001, p. 3)

As one of the two-year-old dictates a one-word story, "Mama," Vivian reflects on her own experience of a one-word story told to her by a boy named Fredrick. His story was simply his name. These one-character stories that are "Mama," or "Fredrick," or "Me, Me, Me, Me, Me," form an early stage in this process that we call storytelling. A character enters the stage. "This is who I am, or this is the character I am pretending to be."

A Scattering of Twos

As I look back over the two-year-olds I have worked with, I notice that they fall into two categories: the settings that contain only a scattering of two-year-olds amongst a group of predominantly three- and four-year-old children; and the ones where I have the luxury of spending time with the two-year-olds on their own. In every case, I find that the pull of the stage means even the most reluctant child grows curious to know what will happen there. Pretty soon, in a room full of two-year-olds, the acting area is filled with children who don't sit down between stories or stay for long within the masking tape lines of the stage.

Where the twos are mixed with older children, they still run onto the stage at every opportunity. The threes and the fours can wait their turn, but the twos revel in the joy of having a part in every story. This is not the age to linger when there are so many experiences to be had.

I remember one time when I had finished leading the acting out of the stories taken on that day from a mixed-age-group of children, and one of the two-year-olds still had the energy for more. He stood up, looked at my piece of paper, and said, "Paw Patrol." Without waiting for me to write his words down, he ran around and around the stage, enjoying the clapping and cheering of his final encore.

These one- or two-word stories mark the beginning of story dictation for many two-year-olds. Unhindered by the structure of storytelling and story acting, they will happily call out the character they want to play and then immediately become it, which happened in Charlotte's first story.

Charlotte – age 2

A big penguin.

Once Charlotte finished her story, she jumped up and began waddling around the stage, her hands held stiffly by her side, her body swaying to and fro. Charlotte knew about penguins, and this was the character she wanted to play.

Like many of the two-year-olds' stories I have scribed, Charlotte's story introduces us to one main character. That is it. There is no more to say. Yet, through her actions, I learn about this character. It waddles across the stage, flapping its flippers. Suddenly our penguin is joined by four other penguins aged two and three years old. Although they were uninvited, they are keen to join in the fun, and who am I to stop them. Charlotte smiles, enjoying the feeling of shuffling back and forth around the stage, followed by her colony.

As Vivian wrote in Mrs Tully's Room, "The two's reach the essence of a scene with the speed of a sprinter." (Paley, 2001, p. 6).

Often early stories will include an action, like Aiysha's or Sofia's below. This drive for movement translates well onto the stage, as our characters can walk or jump, or sit or sleep, or snap like a crocodile. Moving to action is the natural progression from stories that contain only one character. Once we have brought up our cast, we need to work out what they do.

Aiysha – age 2 years 6 months

Mummy walking,
Daddy walking,
Me walking.
Jumping,
Sitting,
Sleeping.

Sofia – age 2 years 6 months

Crocodile.
Snap, snap!

Alone With the Twos

In 2016, I was approached by Tower Hamlets Local Authority to work with a group of two-year-olds in one of their settings. I went with my colleague Isla Hill, and we spent our time telling stories and scribing stories from our young companions.

One of the first stories I scribed was from a boy called Ollie.

Ollie – age 2 years 6 months

Cake.
House.
Eating.
More cake.
Eating.
Cake.

During the acting out, while the other children were miming putting the cake in their mouths, I noticed that Ollie puffed up his cheeks and blew several times before joining the others with the "eating, more cake, eating." The head of the setting whispered to me that Ollie's brother had recently had a birthday. Maybe that's why there was so much cake. But it was Ollie's gesture that fascinated me.

"Ollie, were you blowing out the candles?" I asked.

Ollie puffed up his cheeks and blew and blew and blew. Suddenly all around him, the other children began blowing. For a moment, this group of two-year-olds who spent so much of their time locked into their solo explorations of the world noticed what each other was doing and became a community of actors putting out candles. It shouldn't have surprised me. Story gives us a sense of becoming, of joining together, of being a community, but when this community begins to take shape in the story acting of two-year-olds it is incredible to watch.

"When my babies do their stories, that's when they really see each other," says Lilian Tully… "That's what we need to go after in school, the seeing and the listening to each other."

(Paley, 2001, pp. 11–12)

Vivian Gussin Paley – Personal Correspondence

When you came to Ball State University years ago in order to compare your theater version to my classroom version of this story telling and story acting activity, you placed the connection between play and theater firmly in my mind, as never before.

Over the years, it is the similarity to the theater that has remained both as an explanation and a goal of what I have been doing in a classroom. Play as theater. The classroom as theater. Story dictation as theater.

Every teacher ought to have some training in theater as a part of a general teaching degree program. And this training should include improv and every sort of spontaneous expression. Conformity and control do not represent the spirit of childhood well enough.

Food

Several themes ran through the stories I was told by the two-year-olds in that setting. Often these were linked to the family, or dragons and dinosaurs, but the theme of food was ever-present.

Sergio – age 2

Yum. Yum. Yum.
Yum. Yum. Yum.
My food.
My food.
My food.

As Sergio told me this story, I wondered if my repetition of his words as I wrote them down was responsible for how his story turned out. The scribing went something like this…

Sergio Yum. Yum. Yum.
Me Do you want me to write that down?
Sergio Yes.
Me Yum. Yum. Yum. (I spoke the words out loud as I wrote them.)
Sergio Yum. Yum. Yum.
Me Yum. Yum. Yum. (I said as I wrote.)

Sergio My food.
Me My food. (I said as I wrote.)
Sergio My FOOD!
Me My food. (I said as I wrote.)
Sergio MY FOOD!!!

Realising that Sergio wanted recognition that the food we were talking about was his, I changed my tack. "Your food," I said as I wrote the words "my food" on my piece of paper.

I have had this confusion happen before. Often it arises when a child tells me a story about their family – "my mummy." As I write the words, "my mummy," saying them aloud as I do, the child will frown and say, "MY Mummy." I nod, "Yes, your mummy." Then I return to my page, writing and saying the words "my mummy." And the conversation starts again. Next, we have "My daddy," I repeat the words as I write them down, "My daddy,"

"No, my daddy."

"Yes, your daddy."

The confusion continues like a two-year-old's version of the Abbott and Costello comedy sketch, "Who's on First." When these moments happen, I can see the child processing the notion of ownership and how important this factor is in the story of who they are. The cake is mine, the food is mine, the dinosaur is mine. I am two years old, and I'm staking my claim. The mother I'm imagining is mine, not yours.

Walking and Talking

Often with the two-year-olds, their stories are told while they busily move around, walking and talking. I find myself checking that they want me to write their words down, as sometimes I wonder if I am merely an observer of their play or I feel like I am stealing their words.

Jasper rarely stopped moving. At the start of his spaceman story, he brandished a spoon in the air and triumphantly said the words, "Spaceman. Spaceman. Spaceman."

Jasper – age 2 years 10 months

Spaceman. Spaceman. Spaceman. Spaceman go on a house with a ship. Spaceman never go on house, with a ship, with a tree. A trip on a house with a piece of paper. A spaceman with a spaceship and it cold, and he never needs to drive.

Jasper knocked his spoon on the cupboards as he dictated his story, firing up his space-craft with a whack and a bang. As I repeated his words to write them down, he stopped playing, turned and watched me, waiting till I had finished each sentence before he carried on with his tale. This action reassured me that Jasper wanted me to write his words down.

After a while, Jasper stopped talking. I asked if there was any more to his story. He looked at me, closed his eyes and collapsed against the counter, leaning there for a while as if he had fallen asleep. It was as if he was saying, "What more do you want from me? I have given you my masterpiece. Did you have to ask if it was over?"

The Ability to Imagine in Two-Year-Olds

In his book, *The Work of the Imagination*, Paul L. Harris explores pretend play, naming it one of the earliest indicators of children's developing imagination. He gives the example of an experiment he ran with several two-year-olds, where he placed a teddy bear in a cardboard box, mimed turning on the taps and pretended to wash the teddy's back with a wooden brick. Each of the two-year-olds he worked with readily joined in. The children happily wrapped the teddy in a piece of paper and pretended to dry it. Harris unpicks these episodes, demonstrating how in order to join in with this scenario, the children had to set aside the literal world, where the teddy is in a box, and the soap is a wooden brick. Instead, they buy into the pretend world, where this is a washing scene, and the piece of paper is now a towel. Harris calls this the Suspension of Objective Truth; in theatre, we call it the Suspension of Disbelief. This is where an audience member intentionally avoids critical thinking or stating that something is impossible in order to enjoy and believe in the world of the fiction. We have all done this hundreds of thousands of times without giving it a moment of thought, so it shouldn't be a surprise that this is something young children are capable of.

If the same brick that was once a bar of soap is handed to a two-year-old to feed to the teddy as a sandwich, the child demonstrates flexibility in their imagination, accepting without question the new role assigned to the brick. There is no blocking of the latest scenario. A two-year-old doesn't look at us and say, "Wasn't that the soap a minute ago?" They accept the new version without question. Harris discovered that when the two-year-olds talked about these scenarios later, they referred to the wooden blocks as either soap or sandwiches, depending on which storyline they were discussing.

> It is clear that two-year-olds understand several aspects of a make-believe stipulation. Once a prop has been assigned a make-believe identity... children produce pretend actions towards the prop that exploit the possibilities of its make-believe identity... They also recognise the transient nature of a make-believe stipulation.

In particular, they acknowledge that any new episode opens the way for new make-believe stipulations, which overwrites any stipulations made in previous episodes.

(Harris, 2000, p. 13)

And the More We Nurture It, the Greater Their Imagination Will Grow

Probably one of my favourite stories from a two-year-old comes from a boy named Peter. Peter loved dinosaurs and dragons, and they featured in his tales from his very first story.

Peter – age 2 years 6 months

Flying.
Dinosaur.
Raah!

Over the six weeks that Isla and I worked in Peter's setting, we shared with the children stories we had made up, which they acted out alongside their own stories. The simple stories we created incorporated characters from the stories the children told us: we had dragons flying across the sky, dinosaurs searching for their friends, and girls lost in the forest. In this way, we provided the beginnings of a rich story diet that grew out of the children's own Helicopter Stories.

On the last day in Peter's setting, he dictated the following story.

Peter – age 2 years 7 months

The dragon flew away.
No!
No!
And he's running.

The drama of this story is worthy of any movie set. Sitting on the floor, Peter spread his arms like wings and flapped them slowly up and down while the other children ran around the stage. I will never know who the baddie is in this story or determine whether the man was chasing the dragon or running away. Peter didn't seem to mind. His was the joy of spreading his wings and gently flying, a dragon in the air, unfazed by the impact of his actions on the people he left behind.

Vivian Gussin Paley – Personal Correspondence

Thank you for your dragon story. Most of my dragon stories come from Taiwan, where dragons adorn many of the big buildings. I was sent this one in a recent letter from my friend, Yu-ching, who lives and teaches there.

"Big dragon jumped on a building and it fell down. He ate the building and he jumped to the other building. And he stayed there."

I would say this was an action packed drama. The storyteller is four, and a very quiet child whose mother comes to school with him (not unusual in Taiwan). Unlike American pre-school teachers, in Taiwan the teacher considers it quite normal for a mother to sit against the wall and be available for her young child.

As our babies move towards their third birthday, they have galloped through the early stages of becoming storytellers. They have shown us that they recognise the goodies and the baddies and have a preference for the one they'd like to be. They have suspended their disbelief and entered into a world of pretend. They have also begun to play with language, to appreciate its rhythms and rhymes, alliteration and imagery. As they start to dictate their own stories, they realise that their words are valued, even though they might struggle with the notion of mine and yours. They have transformed from two-year-old children into penguins, spacemen, mummies, and dragons. They have eaten cake, a lot of cake, and strawberries and porridge and toast, and they have pretended to be members of their own families, walking and running around the stage.

> That is why children's oral stories are a fruitful way for us to observe what has been learned, for, in their storytelling, such implicit complexities have the chance to emerge without conscious forethought on the part of the child.
>
> (Carol Fox, 1993, *At The Very Edge of the Forest*, p. 102)

We will leave the twos here, the anarchists of the story world, forever dipping their toes into the world of story. Now they are standing on the yellow brick road, ready to take the next steps in their growth as storytellers.

INTRODUCING THE SECOND TROUPE OF STORYTELLERS

From Three to Four

Actors, writer, storytellers, directors
who took part in the longitudinal study
(in alphabetical order)

Alan, Amelia, Ava, Charlotte,
Chloe, Fleur, Frida, Harper,
Jackson, Layla, Lucas, Madison,
Matteo, Oscar G, Oscar S, Zoe

3 Incredible Connections

"Who are these people who dare to reinvent mythology? They are the children found in every classroom, thinking up plot and dialogue without instruction. And, for the most part, without the teacher's awareness."

Vivian Gussin Paley
(The Boy Who Would Be A Helicopter, p. 4)

DOI: 10.4324/9781003161400-4

When we scribe children's dictated stories, an incredible connection is made between the storyteller and the scribe. This is apparent in how we sit, side by side, the adult writing as the child dictates. We bond over a sheet of A5 paper, tied together by the child's desire to tell us about their world and our longing to hear it. We demonstrate our commitment to this activity in the way that we listen, taking in their words without interrupting. We pay attention, waiting for the scenes to unravel in the child's mind and for their words to form.

But the relationship has two sides. Children demonstrate their commitment to this process too. They choose to stay by our side and not walk away. With three- and four-year-olds, there is no greater proof of their allegiance. In Helicopter Stories, the child wants to tell as much as we want to listen. In the world today, children are largely powerless. When they dictate a story, a child visits a realm where they have control. Telling stories gives them power. It is their chance to put their mark on the world. To make decisions on how they portray their experiences. A child chooses which characters or situations to include in their stories and which ones to leave out. This is their chance to share what matters to them.

As each sentence is dictated, it is fixed as marks on the page. The child sees first-hand the remarkable transformation that happens when a spoken word becomes a written one – another incredible connection. Then they experience longevity. Once their story is in print, it can be shared with a wider audience. It can be looked at over and over again without being forgotten. It can be picked up at the end of the day and shown to a parent or a grandparent. Plus, it can be left in the Nursery, and it will still be there the next day exactly as it was when they told it.

When their stories are acted out, each child goes on to experience other incredible connections. Now written words become spoken words, acted words and moving words, all brought to life by their peers on a taped-out stage. A story that was initially told one-to-one or in the presence of a few friends is shared with the whole class. By allowing their story to be acted out, the storyteller collaborates with the actors, permitting them to represent the characters, objects and situations he or she has created in his or her imagination. The children taking on these roles bring the storytellers' words to life.

But there is also another incredible connection taking place. That is in the impact an acted story has on the children who watch it – the audience. As three- and four-year-olds observe their classmates become characters in a story, they often unconsciously make faces or gestures that are the same as those represented by the actors on the stage. It's as if they are imagining themselves doing the acting and are compelled to mirror the movements or the emotions of the children they are watching. Sometimes in the excitement of a chase scene, a child in the audience might move their arms backwards and forward as if they are the ones who are running. Or they sit with their mouths open, totally engrossed. This pull of the stage is too great for the twos. They will stand up and join in whenever the urge takes them, crawling, or running in a circle or flapping their wings, often with a big smile on their face.

When I watch children of any age, physically and emotionally reacting to the stories told and acted out by their peers, I wonder if their engagement as audience members and the satisfaction this gives them is a part of their drive to become storytellers themselves. Children love watching other children's stories being acted out. Is this what tempts them to tell stories of their own? When children are introduced to Helicopter Stories, it doesn't take long for everyone to want a turn.

In his book, *What Is Literature?* Jean-Paul Sartre said that "as artists, we are compelled to bring our ways of seeing to other human beings…" But what compels our three-and four-years-olds to tell their stories to an adult scribe or to become a character in someone else's story? Do they have this same drive that Sartre suggests to share with others the way they see the world?

From my own experience of delivering Helicopter Stories, I know how vital it is that the stories are acted out. When I first began delivering this approach, I led the acting out REALLY BADLY. I made the mistake of taking fifteen or twenty stories in a session and then not having time to let the children act them. Knowing this, I would select the stories that made it to the stage. Even writing this, I feel sick. But what that time showed me was how important it was for each child to bring his or her story to an audience of their peers. This is the pact we make with a child when we scribe their dictated stories.

In those early days, my approach was a disaster. Week after week, children would ask me when their story (the one that they told a month ago or six weeks ago) would finally get to the stage. They'd remember details about the story that they'd shared with me, even after the longest of time. A four-year-old girl once said to me, "But I want my friends to see it."

I had no idea how to manage storytelling and story acting, so I told the children that maybe this week they could tell me a story, and we would try to act that one out. It was deeply unsatisfying, but I didn't know a better way. Luckily, I saw Vivian Gussin Paley delivering the approach with a group of children after only a few months, and I realised my error. Since then, every story I have scribed has been acted out on the day it was taken. This is one of the hard and fast "rules" that I say in all of my training. But I will never get over the guilt of all those unacted stories that I left behind. Sharing a story with an audience has a massive impact on the storyteller. When we remove this aspect of the approach, we prevent this connection being made.

Vivian Gussin Paley – Personal Correspondence

I feel as if I'm a traveling salesman and my product is doing stories. Funny that it all seems to come down to this activity I prize so highly… After 12 books covering so many other topics, I'm still trying to explain why storytelling and story acting belong in every childhood classroom, and beyond.

The importance of recognizing the natural theater of the young is, I think, spreading here in America. There are pockets of enthusiasts in dozens of places and yet, it is when I come to a group and demonstrate the approach that sparks fly and the teachers are emboldened to see themselves and the children as an acting company.

So I keep traveling.

The Co-created Story

Watch any group of three- and four-year-olds engaged in fantasy play or co-creating a story, and you will see them negotiating their way through the plot. One of them will want the story to go this way, and the other will want it to go in a different direction. Each is compelled to bring their idea of how the story should develop to the other children's attention.

Here are two boys, both called Oscar and a girl named Madison from Bincombe Valley Nursery in Dorset, retelling the story of the Three Little Pigs using some simple wooden toys. They have reached the part where the wolf has the three pigs trapped in the house made of bricks.

OSCAR S Blow the house down.

He knocks his wooden wolf figure against the toy brick house, making it fall over. Madison isn't having any of it. She quickly stands the house up.

MADISON No, it is too strong. That isn't how the story goes.
It's too strong.
It's too strong.
It's too strong.

Oscar S finds another way to get around the problem.

OSCAR S I'll climb on the roof and go through the chimney.

Madison blocks him, reminding him of the plot.

MADISON In the hot water.
In the chimney.

Oscar G, who has been watching, quietly all this time, suddenly speaks, siding with Madison on the purity of the story.

OSCAR G Light the fire.

Madison and Oscar G busily move their hands behind the wooden brick house, getting the fire ready.

MADISON I got the fire on.
OSCAR G He's on the fire.

But Oscar S has other ideas. He's not ready to burn yet.

OSCAR S He jumped over it.
MADISON No! No, you need to go in the fire.

Madison is determined. The fate of the story hangs in the balance.

OSCAR S He jumped over it.

Oscar S won't give up without a fight. There's a pause as all three children look for help from the teacher who is filming them.

TEACHER Well, maybe in your story, maybe he could jump over the fire and run away. Maybe it is a different ending.

Madison is happy with the compromise. She calls the wolf to get back on the roof, offering him the chance to try out a different version, as suggested by the teacher.

MADISON Come back up here.

But Oscar S has another idea.

OSCAR S He jumps off the roof.
And he hurts himself.
And he runs away.

Oscar S is satisfied. Madison resigned. The story comes to an end.

Each of the three children above has their own version of how the story should play out, but they have to find a way to compromise as the story-making is shared. When children play together, they either insist that the story goes their way and that everyone else has to fit in with them, or they learn to negotiate. The art of negotiation is an essential part of dramatic play. Without it, the story can't move forward. Some disagreements can be resolved by children working together to tweak their ever-evolving scripts. Others rely on one or more children agreeing to let go of their own ideas and accept those put forward more forcefully.

However, when a child is dictating his or her own story, they get to make all the decisions independently. Here is an opportunity for the individual to present their unique "ways of seeing" to others without negotiating with anyone.

Vivian Gussin Paley – Personal Correspondence

I remember once, when I was demonstrating storytelling and story acting in a private school in Manhattan, a first grade girl who lived on the 16th floor of a high rise, told me, "all my stories will be about very little houses."

"Why is that?" I asked.

"Because my mind is in a little house," she said.

When we acted her story I told the other children what she had said and everyone agreed.

"Little houses are best."

The Themes That Connect Us

When a two-year-old tells a one-word story, "Mummy," all the other two-year-olds start thinking about their Mummy, how she behaves and what sort of activities she does. Likewise, when a three-year-old tells a story about dinosaurs, all the information the listening children have about dinosaurs, lights up in their brain. This enables them to imagine how a dinosaur moves, and to either portray this character as an actor or project a make-believe image of this character onto another child as they watch from the audience.

But it is not just the characters a story contains that connects it to the other children. The emotions also resonate with the audience.

> # Frida – age 3
>
> The girl.
> And they gone now.
> Her go home.
> Go home.

When I worked with Frida, she was three years old. She had only been at the Nursery a couple of weeks. Her four-year-old cousin was in the same group as her, and she could often be found sitting next to him or walking so close to him that she'd almost trip him up. In those early days, Frida didn't say a lot. She watched, her brown eyes taking in everything as she stood by her cousin, waiting to follow wherever he went. Frida's early stories consist of just one word.

> Daddy – 7 November 2019
> Dragon – 28 November 2019
> Daddy – 12 December 2019
> Crocodile – 30 January 2020
> Daddy – 6 February 2020

Daddy was hugely significant. As Frida walked around the stage, pretending to be him, she always had a big grin on her face.

Over the four months that it took Frida to tell me these stories, she also made a new friend, Amma. No longer did she stay by her cousin's side. Now Frida and Amma went everywhere together. They mirrored each other's movements, one finger in their mouth, the other hand tangled in their hair. They whispered to each other and shared secrets and smiles that had no need for words.

Then, in late February 2020, just before the first UK Covid-19 Lockdown, Amma and her family moved away. The story at the top of this chapter is the last story Frida told me before Covid-19 prevented me from visiting her setting. She dictated it slowly, her words weighted with sadness. "The girl. And they gone now. Her go home. Go home." This was a love poem to a friend who had left, from the one who stayed behind.

Frida frowned as she told her story, trying to understand this strange new world in which Amma was no longer around. She took the role of the girl when we acted the story out as if playing the character of Amma would help her make sense of what had happened. As the acting started, Frida walked in circles forlornly around the stage. It was then that I saw the depth of her emotion. She seemed lost. Alone. I wanted the other children to build a house with their bodies so I could place Frida safely inside, but it was a day full of two-year-olds and just-turned three-year-olds, and the children had their own ideas.

When I read the words "Her go home," I asked the other children if they could pretend to be a house for the girl to sit inside. They ignored me, preferring to walk around the stage, following Frida, their faces equally as sad. Perhaps they sensed that she was where the heart of this story lay, and they didn't need to fulfil my vision of a girl sitting in a house.

The children continued to follow Frida, their faces sad, walking around and around the stage like a scene from the Pied Piper. Eventually, we clapped thank you, and the story came to an end. I wasn't sure if Frida even noticed the other children. She seemed trapped in her own thoughts, and as soon as the story ended and her truth had been shared, she sat by her cousin and stayed by his side for the rest of the morning.

The emotions contained in Frida's story connected with everyone in the room. From a very early age, we understand this type of pain. We might have cried when we were left by our parents for the very first time or when a friend had to go home. Love and loss: these are universal themes, and yet three-year-old Frida manages to conveys these emotions in eleven words.

> If we manage to persuade children to tell stories fairly often, we may find that linguistic, narrative and literary competences of very complex kinds are revealed to us, competencies that are not so readily observable in other forms of child discourse.
>
> (Carol Fox, 1993, *At The Very Edge Of The Forest*, p. 8)

The creative way young children tell their stories, their brevity with words often provides depth and pathos that wordier writing might miss. A good storyteller leaves room for the listener to layer their own emotions onto the narrative. Frida's story gets straight to the point; her friend is gone. The end of the story is punctuated by her repetition of the word "go." This serves to emphasise the emotions. There's also a melancholy tone to this story, which Frida's use of short sentences enhances. This is the poetry of a three-year-old encased in sadness.

Vivian Gussin Paley – Personal Correspondence

Here is a story from a four year old in Edmonton, Canada.
   "There was a Princess and she was picking flowers. But she dropped them and the petals came off. And someone came and put back every petal."
   Of course we had to ask who came. The answer was "a friend".
   "Yes," I said. "A friend is the someone who puts the petals back on for you."

In his book *Imagination and Creativity in Childhood*, Vygotsky says, "A child's play is not simply a reproduction of what he has experienced, but a creative reworking of the impressions he has acquired." In her story, Frida shares her creative reworkings of an experience she has had and the impression it left her with. She reveals her emotions about her friend's disappearance, allowing us as her audience to not only experience it but to contribute our own emotions too.

So much is achieved in such a few short words. But this is not the shortest story ever told.

The Shortest Story Ever

Apparently, or so the rumour goes, American novelist Ernest Hemingway was at a bar in the 1920s when he entered into a bet with some fellow writers. He wagered that he could write a complete story, one that would give his audience an emotional connection, in only six words. Hemingway said that if he succeeded, the other writers would have to pay him ten dollars each. But if he failed, he would give each of them ten dollars. That was a lot of money in the 1920s. Fortunately for Hemingway, he won the bet. Within minutes of shaking on the deal, he wrote the following story on a napkin and passed it around the table.

FOR SALE,
BABY SHOES,
NEVER WORN.

These six words are famous for being the shortest story ever told. There are some people who doubt that the bet actually took place and others who question whether this six-word story can be credited to Hemingway. However, the reality is, it doesn't matter. Whatever the truth behind its origin, the six-word story tells a fully rounded tale. It includes a beginning, a middle and an end, and we fill in the gaps when we read the story.

Why are the baby shoes for sale when they have never been worn? Our instinct is to make sense of these words, to bring this story to life in our heads, so we fill in the gaps. We assume that something tragic has happened to the baby. We feel sad. In this shortest of stories, we experience a world where a baby died before it even had the chance to wear its first pair of shoes.

If it is good enough for Ernest Hemingway to be credited with having written a story in six words, then it is good enough for three-year-old Frida from Chippenham to offer us her view on love and loss in this eleven-word epic.

What Makes a Good Story?

As I journey into the growth of a storyteller and revisit the stories that children have shared with me over the past few years, I find myself in awe of the creativity they demonstrate. But what makes a good story? Do our three- and four-year-olds' dictated stories contain any of the characteristics that we would recognise as great if they were present in something written by an adult?

Any good writing course will say that one of the critical ingredients to make a story connect with us is by having a great opening line. This first line of a story gives us a sense of what it contains. It is the moment when we enter the story world, and in one or two sentences, we are presented with a situation where we want to know more.

Most stories start at a point of change, at a time in our protagonist's life when he or she is facing something new. There is often a sense of trepidation about what the future holds. This is sophisticated stuff that would-be writers fixate on, trying to find that killer opening line that will hook our readers and make our stories irresistible.

But young storytellers have no such anxieties. They dive in with the speed of a peregrine falcon and unravel their stories effortlessly.

In Frida's short story, we arrive at a moment of change in the main character's life. She had a friend, and now her friend is gone. "The girl. And they gone now." The hook draws us in. We want to know what happens. Is it a tragedy, or does her story have a happy ending?

Here are some famous opening lines from children's literature.

Where the Wild Things Are

The night Max wore his wolf suit and made mischief of one kind, and another his mother called him "WILD THING!" and Max said "I'LL EAT YOU UP!" so he was sent to bed without eating anything.

We arrive as Max has been sent to bed without supper. An event outside of the normal has happened, Max is in trouble, and we want to know what happens next.

Where's Spot?

That Spot! He hasn't eaten his supper. Where can he be?

From this opening sentence, we know that something has happened to Spot. He hasn't eaten his dinner, and no one has seen him.

Peter Pan

All children, except one, grow up.

As we read this opening line, we are curious to know about the child who doesn't grow up. What is his story?

Charlotte's Web

"Where's Papa going with that axe?" said Fern to her mother as they were setting the table for breakfast.

Papa has an axe, and because Fern is asking about it, we know that this doesn't happen regularly. This is something that needs to be investigated.

In each of these opening lines, we are launched into the world of the story at a moment of change, and we're intrigued to know more. But these are adult writers. Can three- and four-year-olds really give us opening lines as sophisticated as this?

In the box below, I share the beginnings of six stories told to me by three children, Zoe, Fleur and Matteo. The stories were told when the children were aged three and four.

The First Line of a Story by 3- and 4-year-olds

Zoe – age 3

The dog crashed a plate and a cake.

Fleur – age 3

Once a fairy walked over a roof.

Matteo – age 3

A volcano. It explodes.

Zoe – age 4

Once there was a rabbit who lost its ball in the fog.

Fleur – age 4

The dinosaur chased Mummy.

Matteo – age 4

One day had a secret cave.

Any of these opening lines would not be out of place at the start of a professionally published story by an adult. These are not highly literate children from an affluent area. They are three- and four-year-olds from one of the most impoverished districts in Wiltshire. But none of this stops them. Children's natural ability to leap straight into a story often means that their opening lines are highly compelling.

But where does this ability come from? Lisa Cron, in her book, *Wired for Story*, believes that as humans, we are wired to recognise a good story quickly, from the very first sentence; and that children are capable of this from a young age. Cron expands her theory by looking at the history of evolution and demonstrating how this urge to listen to a good story might save our life. "Don't eat those shiny red berries. Let me tell you what happened to the last person who ate them." According to Lisa Cron, the sentence we open with is vital in drawing the audience in before we begin with the rest of our tale.

Vivian Gussin Paley – Personal Correspondence

If I were to choose a single classroom experience to counteract the adverse effects of the electronic age I would pick storytelling and story acting.

It is the first activity to be set aside and yet it holds within its power the soul of the child and the intimacy of language and dreams.

Someone Else's Shoes

In the previous chapter, I wrote about Charlotte. At two years old, she demonstrated how story gives us the ability to step into someone else's shoes, or with Charlotte's penguin story, into her character's webbed feet. This notion of stepping into someone else's shoes is one of the ways a story connects with us, both as the creator of the story and as the audience.

Imagine a three-year-old saying to her friend, "You be the baby, I'll be the mum, and the mum is cross." As the three-year-old is speaking, she wags her finger and takes on the role of the cross Mum. In this way, the child steps into Mum's shoes and finds out what it feels like to be a Mum who is cross. She explores the question, "How would I act if I was feeling like that?"

All of us who have spent any time around young children will have seen something like this. It might be the child who pretends to take the register with precisely the same mannerisms as the teacher or the one who's talking on an imaginary telephone using exactly the same tone and phrasing as we have often used ourselves.

A child I worked with many years ago used to put her hands on her hips, and moving her head backwards and forward, she'd say in a sassy voice, "Just you wait, young lady." Watching her mimicry, all of us could picture the adult she was imitating. The role made the little girl feel powerful. This was evident from the delight in her expression. But she also experienced the enjoyment of the performer and the pleasure of sharing her impression of Mum with an audience.

Stepping into someone else's shoes helps develop our empathy, our sense of right and wrong, our emotional intelligence. But what is happening inside our brain?

The Story of Phineas Gage

Until the mid-1970s, when the first (MRI) magnetic resonance imaging machines were introduced, the primary way to study the brain was by removing it after somebody had died. If a scientist wanted to understand where speech, emotions, or memory were located in the brain, they had to find someone who had damaged one of these areas and then wait until that person died to remove their brain and find out where the damage was located.

Through this inquiry-based approach in 1848, scientists discovered that our sense of right or wrong, our moral compass, has a biological place in our brain. This discovery is attributed to an accident involving a railway construction worker, Phineas Gage. Phineas was responsible for blasting holes in the rock to make railway tunnels until something went wrong.

The explosive nitroglycerin had been set, but while Phineas was still backing away, the blast went off early. Shooting out of the rock came a long metal rod, headed straight towards him. As he glanced back in horror, the rod pushed its way underneath Phineas's left eye, through his brain and shot out from the top of his head, landing several feet away, smeared with blood and brain.

Incredibly, following treatment, Phineas survived for twelve years after his accident, suffering very few physical effects. Once the healing had taken place, he could walk, move around and continue his everyday life practically the same as before.

However, friends who worked with Phineas Gage said that after the accident, his personality changed dramatically. He was previously a mild-mannered man; afterwards, he was reported to indulge in "the grossest of profanities." He swore profusely, was rude to his friends and his sense of empathy towards them was significantly reduced. The accident altered Phineas's moral compass. The piercing of his frontal lobe had somehow interrupted his ability to judge how to behave in different situations, to care for others, to sense what was right and wrong. He had lost the ability to consider his friends' reactions when he behaved in a certain way.

We may know someone who struggles with this, who has problems stepping outside of their own needs to become aware of the needs of others. We learn this, well most of us do, often through making mistakes or upsetting people and realising there is a kinder way to behave. Stories can help us to understand this.

A Bad Day

Lance, one of the Reception children I worked with as part of the longitudinal study, once told me a story about the Incredible Hulk. Lance's portrayal of Hulk's anger reminds me of the difficulties Phineas Gage had in controlling his emotions.

Lance – age 5

Hulk was on his motorbike. Then he broke it and forgot his keys. Then he crashed his motorbike because he was angry. Then someone comed, and he punched them. Then he went to the park so he could punch all the people. Then he wanted to crash all over the park.

This story demonstrates the gap between what is acceptable in real life and what is allowed to happen in a story. The Hulk is having a bad day. He takes revenge on everyone he meets, and in Lance's version, he gets away with it. Hulk has no remorse, and unlike the TV drama, he doesn't have to go back into hiding or feel sad about what he has done. This is pure rage at what life has thrown at him.

As Lance scribed his story, his face screwed up with pretend anger. He is usually a quiet child who doesn't speak much to adults. The story was in contrast to his everyday demeanour, and he was enjoying it.

In real life, we learn from an early age that it is not acceptable to act out our frustration. When we feel anger, we are told to calm down, take a deep breath and hold it all in. How satisfying for a five-year-old to play out a different way to deal with emotions, an angry way, where you can stomp and punch and yell in the safe knowledge that it is only pretend.

When Lance acted out this story, he took on the role of the Hulk. I can still picture him snarling and growling as he mimed punching and stomping his feet. The children in the audience were fixated on the stage; this was a side to Lance that they had never seen before. One of them cheered, a couple laughed and several had their fist clenched and were pretending to punch alongside him. For a brief moment, Lance was able to be angry, and the audience got to experience the world from an angry person's perspective. Both audience and actor/writer had a cathartic experience, they got rid of some of their anger in a pretend way, leaving it on the stage when the story was over.

The more we experience different characters' viewpoints, the more we develop that same part of our brain that Phineas Gage damaged so severely. This is the Science of Story.

The Brain Lights Up

Over the last few years, neurologists have become increasingly interested in the impact that storytelling has on the brain, and more is still being learned about this. What is known is that when we engage in story, our brains light up.

Have you ever watched a film or read a book that made you cry? That is your Temporal Lobe, the part that is responsible for governing your emotions sparking into life. The reason for this is because, as the person receiving the story, you are so engaged with the character that you're crying your own tears for them. The writer was also engaged with the character, so their Temporal Lobe would have lit up as they wrote. If the story is a film, the actor would also have engaged with the character. Therefore, to portray that level of emotion, the actor's Temporal Lobe would have lit up in the same way too.

Thinking about all those connections, those similarities in the way our brains respond as creators, performers and audience, it is no wonder this stuff is so powerful.

When I watch the film *Titanic*, which I have seen several times, there is one moment near the end of the film when I find it hard not to cry.

The ship is going down. Rose is lying on a bit of wood. Jack is beside her in the water. He's freezing, exhausted and needs to keep holding onto the wood to stay alive.

"Don't let go," says Rose.

But of course, Jack lets go.

When I watch this part of the story, part of my brain thinks, "Come on, Rose, move over so Jack can climb on." That's my Neocortex trying to solve the problem. Then another part, my Temporal Lobe, is responsible for me crying my eyes out. While I am watching, I know I am safe. I'm sat on my settee, at home, but a large part of me feels like it is there, in the water, watching a loved one die. I might reach out like Rose to try to save Jack from drowning or hold my breath for Jack. That is my Motor Cortex lighting up. It is as though what is physically happening to the character is physically happening to me too. I might even back away from the telly, which is my Amygdala telling me it is not safe.

I have just described in the most simplistic of terms only a tiny part of what is happening in our brains when we engage in the story, and this will keep changing at different times during the film. That is an awful lot of lighting up. (If there are any neurologists reading, I apologise as I am sure it's more complex than this, but this is a summary of how I understand it.)

When we receive a story, we might feel embarrassed about crying or reacting fearfully, but we don't need to. These are moments of human connection, incredible connections, where everyone's brain is lighting up in the same way, the writer, the actor, the audience member. What amazes me is that these connections happen, whether we are watching a blockbuster by Paramount Pictures or we are a group of three- and four-year-olds watching or taking part in a story about the Incredible Hulk.

Hearts Beat as One

In 2017, University College London (UCL) invited several audience members of a show called *Dream Girls* at the Savoy Theatre to take part in an experiment. They selected participants from across the auditorium. None of the participants knew each other. Before the show started, UCL researchers wired the participants up to heart monitors so that they could monitor their heartbeats during the performance.

The researchers noted that before the show started, everyone's heart had its own individual beat, and it was impossible to draw any relationship between them. This makes sense. When we walk into a room, our hearts don't synchronise with everyone present.

However, as the performance began and the audience emotionally engaged with the story, the heartbeats of everyone who was being monitored across the whole auditorium started to beat at exactly the same speed. When the action in the story heated up, everyone's heartbeat sped up, all at exactly the same time. As the storyline relaxed, the heartbeats of the audience slowed.

After the show, UCL researchers were able to track the highs and lows of the storyline by looking across all the monitors and noting the speed of the audience members' hearts in response to what was happing on the stage. How remarkable, an audience of theatre-goers, all with their hearts beating as one.

But it's not just in the theatre that our hearts synchronise. It happens when we share stories. It's that moment when we are completely in tune with the people around us. When everyone is focused and believing in the world of the story and rooting for the main character. When we're thinking and working as one. Like children during Helicopter Stories, we are somehow incredibly connected.

4 The Ordinary World

"The stories flow in unbounded variety, and no first-time story is the same as any other. The three year olds listen to the daily accumulation of stories, but when the spirit finally moves the new storyteller, it is invariably a unique event."

Vivian Gussin Paley
(*Mollie is Three*, p. 60)

DOI: 10.4324/9781003161400-5

Human beings have shared stories with each other for over 150,000 years. We've painted them on the walls of caves, recited them as poems and spoken them in hushed tones around glowing fires. We have written them in books and presented them on big screens. We have acted them in theatres and shared them with our friends over cups of coffee. Stories are present in everything we do. They make us human. In his book, *The Science of Storytelling*, Will Storr said,

> There's simply no way to understand the human world without stories. They fill our newspapers, our law courts, our sporting arenas, our government debating chambers, our school playgrounds, our computer games, the lyrics to our songs, our private thoughts and public conversations and our waking and sleeping dreams. Stories are everywhere. Stories are us.
>
> (Storr, 2019, p. 2)

With narrative taking up such an enormous part of our everyday lives, it is hardly surprising that young children are such experts in this field and can invent the most remarkable stories. Sadly, it is far too easy to miss these gems in a climate where the pressure to formalise Early Years education results in children having less time for play, and for all the benefits that accompany this. Today's children have less time to plot their escape from a dragon, or to look after the poorly kitten, or rescue the good Knight from the monster. There is less time to explore the things that are important to them, in a world where the rules are their own. The sad reality of nowadays is, children are rarely listened to by adults. I don't mean acknowledging what they say; I mean really listened to, where we, as grownups, don't feel the need to interrupt, offer guidance or teach and where everything the child says is valued. When we scribe and act out stories regularly, we demonstrate to the child our respect and willingness to listen. In return, we discover an openness on the part of the child to share with us their deepest thoughts, the play-fulness of their language, the metaphors they're inventing, and the humour and wisdom they hold. The results are incredibly rewarding.

Vivian Gussin Paley – Personal Correspondence

We too in America must work hard to counter the misconceptions and indifference of policy workers who value early lessons as a replacement for play.

I'm to speak to the US Department of Education, to Early Childhood Directors and Policy Makers. I'll talk about fantasy play and the fact that it's fast disappearing from our schools. Most people in charge of schools would rather not be reminded.

Play is so messy and loud, their workbooks are neat and visible and controlled. Perhaps I'll remind them of what fantasy play is all about and why it's a shame to be losing the knack of it in our schools. I'll start with a warning story of my own, perhaps.

The Poetry of Children

When I listen to the dictated stories of three- and four-year-olds, it amazes me how often the form they use to express themselves is akin to poetry. The earliest stories ever told were written as epic poems. Poetic language works well in an oral culture. The use of rhythm and rhyme helps storytellers to remember long sequences of events as well as making them more memorable to their audience. Obviously, the stories young children dictate cannot be reflected upon in the same vein as the epic poem *Gilgamesh* created in 2100 BCE. Still, children's ability to play with rhythm and rhyme and use repetition to emphasise their point demonstrates their ability to think poetically, even while they are still in the process of mastering speech.

Three- and four-year-olds are pre-literate. In the same way as the ancient Mesopotamians from 6,000 years ago, they are developing their use of language. There is no proven link between the evolution of epic poetry in Mesopotamia and the inclusion of rhythm and rhyme in the stories dictated by many three-year-olds, but I find the similarities fascinating. It is a tremendous achievement for a young mind to place into story form all the bits of linguistic knowledge they have acquired so far. Yet, somehow, our three- and four-year-olds construct meaning and insert poetry into their dictated stories with unconscious ease.

In 1928, Russian children's poet Kornei Chukovsky published a book about his observations on the poetry contained in children's early language development. Many of his opinions mirror my experiences from the stories I have heard children tell.

> There is hardly a child who does not go through a stage in his pre-school years when he is not an avid creator of word rhythms and rhymes.
>
> (Kornei Chukovsky, 1974, *From Two to Five*, p. 64)

Some examples of this type of poetry can be seen in the stories below, dictated by Fleur and Chloe at the start of their growth as storytellers.

Fleur – age 3

A broken train,
A broken man,
A broken book.
The girl wake up,
A broken puppy,
A broken cup.

Chloe – age 3

Cat get off the mat.
Cat get off the cat.
Cat saw spider,
Then she runned away.

Fleur's repetition of the word "broken" creates the rhythm that runs through her story. Then in the fourth sentence, she breaks away from this. The girl wakes up. This feels like sophisticated poetry because Fleur immediately returns to the rhythm repeating her "broken" stanza another two times. She also rhymes "The girl wake up" with "The broken cup." This use of rhythm and rhyme creates a poem that feels deeply satisfying to the reader. Likewise, in Chloe's story, there are moments of rhyme – the mat, the cat. There is also a rhythm that works over a beat of five that runs through the length of her story. On the third line, this rhythm changes, but because we return to the beat of five on the final line, the poem feels complete.

Now I am not saying that these are child geniuses who have worked out stanzas and rhythm. None of this is deliberate. This is children playing with language, enjoying the sounds of words and the pleasure of rhythm and rhyme. Humans have been playing in this way for thousands of years. In the womb, a baby is surrounded by the sound of their mother's heartbeat. As they grow, they hear nursery rhymes and songs. All of these influences shape our desire to experiment with language in this way. It is time we recognised that children are capable of creating poetry through their spoken words, yet it is so easy to miss this if we don't scribe their stories regularly.

However, it is not just the ability to use language poetically that we witness in children's stories. We also get to find out how they think. In the world of make believe, children go on incredible adventures. They become weird and wonderful characters. But more importantly, they also get to decide the rules, the "who, where, what and how" of their story world. When a child tells a story, they exert their control over the world of that story and decide on the laws that govern it. For children who are regularly given this level of autonomy through Helicopter Stories, the results can be spectacular.

Harper – age 4

The ten little cats and the big bad bowl. And then all the different cats and kittens got stuck in jail. And they were stuck forever, and a Superhero did not save them.

In the story above, Harper, a girl with learning difficulties and suspected ADHD, bestows an inanimate object with a personality – the big bad bowl. Harper knows about the big bad wolf, but for her, there is more fun to be had when she defies our expectations. Let's change the wolf into a bowl and see what happens. Later in the story, Harper again refuses to give us what we expect. This is a story where nothing is as it seems, and even a superhero won't save us.

When the story was acted out, Harper became the Big Bad Bowl. She sat on the masking tape stage, her arms forming a circle in front of her, while she growled at any of the kittens who came near. Harper understood the humour of her story. Her eyes laughed at the mischievousness of it all, demonstrating her self-awareness at how the story was being perceived. By creating a world where bowls growl, and superheroes don't rescue you, Harper revealed something of the chaos of her existence. In real life, Harper was always getting told off for doing things differently. However, when she dictates a story, she knows that the adult will accept whatever she says. Harper's story world is a place where she makes the decisions. The girl who refuses to conform in real life creates an imaginative, funny nonconforming story that demonstrates far more about her potential than any educational test could reveal.

Abstract Thinking

When children act out their stories, they share with us their ability to think abstractly, shaping their bodies to represent objects they have seen in the physical world, just like Harper did when she became the big bad bowl. It is worth noticing the intricacy of the detail that children include in their acting out when they become animals, monsters or buildings. They might show us their claws, their facial expressions or even their overall shape. A five-year-old I worked with decided to become a house by placing both his hands and feet on the ground and then lifting one foot into the air with a bended knee to represent the chimney. As an adult invited to do the same, we may have gone for a safer, more conventional option, perhaps shaping our hands to form a triangle. I would never have thought to use my body in such an imaginative way. Yet, there was accuracy and creativity to this five-year-old's abstract thinking that satisfied the audience so much that for months afterwards, the only way this group of five-year-olds would pretend to be a house was by making exactly the same shape.

So where does this ability for abstract thinking come from?

In 2019, a group of archaeologists in Indonesia uncovered paintings on the walls of a cave that they believed were the first artwork ever to depict a fictitious story. The painting was fourteen feet long and contained a hunting scene filled with supernatural beings with birds' heads and long tails hunting pigs and buffalos. The archaeologists believe that this 45,000-year-old painting is the earliest example of humans demonstrating their capacity for symbolic representation. The artists who created the cave painting had the mental capacity to imagine creatures and situations that do not exist in this world and to represent this in pictures.

> "It's quite amazing. It's a narrative scene, and it's the first time we see that in the rock art," says the study author Maxime Aubert, who is an archaeologist at Griffith University in Australia… "The humans there, they are not fully human: one has a tail, then others may have some sort of bird's head or something," he says. "I think it's probably something that didn't really exist. Maybe it's part of a mythical creature."
>
> (Independent Newspaper, 18 December 2019)

According to the study, the presence of these half-human, half-bird creatures indicates that the artists were thinking abstractly and creatively. This ability to make up stories, to create a narrative scene was described by Maxime Aubert as "one of the last steps of human cognition."

Isn't it amazing that this massive leap forward for humanity, this celebration of the last steps of human cognition, is something our preschool children are doing regularly without any intervention from us? And they do this despite all the pressures and restrictions of our modern society. Surely then, it is vital we take the time to value it.

Sophisticated Storytellers

When we listen to our young storytellers, the sophistication of what they are capable of is revealed to us. Children think abstractly, they use irony, speak poetically and are filled with humour. By tuning in to children's dramatic play, we discover that our pre-schools are full of cats, kittens, unicorns, fairies, dragons, tigers, snakes, lions, crocodiles, wolves, butterflies and an assortment of other animals, people and objects ready to show us the world from the storytellers' perspective. These characters run away, fall over, fly, eat, get eaten, get ill, get broken, get scared, get chased, get lost. They die and come back to life again, and they exist in the child's imagination. When we scribe children's stories, we see how these characters and events are revisited and reinvented time and time again by children who seem compelled to occupy themselves in this way.

> There is no activity for which young children are better prepared than fantasy play. Nothing is more dependable and risk-free, and the dangers are only pretend.
>
> (Vivian Gussin Paley, 2004, *A Child's Work*, p. 8)

Stories occupy a crucial role in our evolution. They enable us to imagine what the future might look like and the steps we can take to make it better. They draw us in without us even realising that we've become engrossed. In her book, *Wired for Story* (2012, p. 1), Lisa Cron says, "The pleasure we derive from a tale well-told is nature's way of seducing us into paying attention."

But what is it that we choose to pay attention to?

Research by evolutionary psychologist Robin Dunbar suggests that two-thirds of our conversation is taken up by us sharing information on who is doing what to whom and why. He believes that story has its origin in gossip and argues that as social animals, we are fascinated by the "interests and minutiae of everyday social life." Dunbar points out that this is reflected in the type of books we choose to read, with the quantity of fiction published and sold every year, topping the bestselling book lists high above non-fiction. In his book, *Grooming, Gossip and the Evolution of Language* (1996, p. 5), Dunbar says that we are captivated by the "unfolding intimacies of the main characters. It is the way they handle their experiences that fascinates us," and that our desire to learn what the world is like from another person's viewpoint is an essential part of how we survive in communities.

> Indeed, Homo sapiens conquered this planet thanks above all to the unique human ability to create and spread fictions. We are the only mammals that can cooperate with numerous strangers because only we can invent fictional stories, spread them around, and convince millions of others to believe in them. As long as everybody believes in the same fictions, we all obey the same laws and can thereby cooperate effectively.
>
> (Yuval Noah Harari, 2018, *21 Lessons for the 21st Century*, p. 233)

The Personal Story

When we see how characters in fiction deal with the issues that face them, it enables us to examine the issues in our own lives. Likewise, when we share our personal stories with a friend or colleague, we check in with each other and discover if our experiences are similar to those around us. We learn from each other, and this stops us from feeling alone.

> Story originated as a method of bringing us together to share specific information that might be lifesaving.
>
> (Lisa Cron, 2012, *Wired for Story*, p. 3)

Let's suppose I had a bad accident, and I needed to go into hospital to have shoulder replacement surgery. (In case any of you are worried, this isn't something that has happened to me, but it has happened to someone in my family, so I know quite a bit about it.) So, imagine that I have severely damaged my shoulder, the ball joint has broken away from my arm, this is nasty stuff, and the only option open to me is to have it replaced. What do I do? Probably I'd talk with one of my friends about it. By doing this, I would be looking to ease my anxiety, to share my fear about what has happened to me. I would also be hoping for empathy or reassurance from the other person.

But supposing my friend surprised me with her reply.

"Oh, that happened to my mum."

Suddenly, I'd find myself engaged in a conversation, talking about the similarities and the differences between my experiences and those of my friend's Mum. I would learn from my friend the things that went well.

"Mum was out of hospital in a few days. She was in very little pain."

But I might also learn about something I needed to look out for.

"Make sure you do the exercises they give you. My Mum didn't do them, and she still can't lift her arm very high."

From this chance conversation, I have received reassurance that someone else has experienced a similar situation to me, but I have also been given a warning of what could happen if I don't keep up with the physio. The story my friend shares gives me a greater understanding of how things could turn out.

This sharing of personal stories takes place in both adults and children. When a four-year-old falls and cuts him- or herself – after the tears have dried and the scab has formed – you might hear him or her showing the wound to a friend and comparing injuries. As a result of this human compulsion to talk about things that have happened to us, it is to be expected that personal events and experiences will also find their way into children's dictated stories.

Amelia, whose stories I scribed many years ago, was a girl who loved to climb. She climbed everything, and height was never a barrier. Often, she fell, and she was always covered in bruises, but this didn't deter her. The first story I scribed for Amelia told me everything I needed to know about her love of climbing.

Amelia – age 4

The girl climb up.
And her fell, and her hurt her arm.
There was a bump and a bruise.
Mummy pick the girl up.
And the girl climb up the slide.

Amelia's story shows that she is aware that she falls over a lot, but it also told me that this didn't bother her. She ends her story as she does in life, climbing the next big object.

When we acted the story out, Amelia played herself. She didn't want to be the Mum, picking the girl up and fussing around her. Amelia wanted to show the world that she was okay. How even though she had fallen time and time again, she was still ready to climb. As Amelia mimed putting one hand in front of the other as she made her way up the dangerous part of the slide, I could see the joy that climbing gave her.

But it is not just the bruises that appear in children's stories; the whole spectrum of human life has the potential to weave its way in.

Alan – age 3

> BBBBLLLLL.
> Boy sick.

When Alan dictated the story above, he put his hands up to his face and made the sound of being sick. "BBBBLLLLL." I asked if he wanted me to write it down. He nodded. Then he put his mouth close to my ear and whispered, "boy sick." So I wrote that down too. There was no more to Alan's story, but of course, this was enough; that simple gesture and those two words told me why he had been off school for the last few days. When we came to act out Alan's story, he stood on the stage and made the same gesture of being sick into his hands, accompanied by the sound. Then he paused with comic genius, frozen in the image whilst I read the words, "Boy sick."

The class laughed and laughed, and Alan stood proudly, soaking up the applause. One of the parents popped her head around the door to find out what the noise was, but it was beyond explanation. It was one of those rare comic moments where timing is everything, and only those present were part of the experience. The laughter was empathetic. We all know what it's like to be sick, and because the sharing of this experience involved humour, we saw the funny side of something that happens to us all.

But the stories children tell about things that happen in their lives aren't always that literal. Sometimes, it is only by reading between the lines and knowing what is going on for the child that you can decipher the meaning.

Milly had leukaemia at the age of two and has spent a lot of her early childhood in hospital. The leukaemia had an impact on her heart, and although she is healthy most of the time, about once a year, she ends up spending a few weeks in hospital. One of these incidences happened while I was working in her Year 2 classroom. I was present on the day she returned from an extended stay in hospital. Here is the story she dictated.

Milly – age 7

Once upon a time, there was seventeen children in a class doing work. There were seventeen names. Some of them were Benji, Hannah, Ethan and Hayley. Then they went out for playtime. After playtime, they had lunch and music. And then they had science and fruit, and it was home time. Then they went back to school to go on an adventure. Then they all went home to have a glass of milk and breakfast in bed. They slept in bed and had a nice dream about letters.

Although it is not evident from the story above, Milly is an avid storyteller, often telling stories rich in fairy tale characters and imagination. This story stood out for its blandness. It is a story of the everyday, the boring, the routine. But of course, it makes sense. Milly had had her adventure. She'd been seriously ill. This story of routine and familiarity is a fantastic example of the role story played in Milly's life. It might even have been the story she told herself when she was in hospital, imagining what her friends were doing at various points of the day. When the adventure of reality became too much for Milly, the mundane of the ordinary offered comfort.

Vivian Gussin Paley – Personal Correspondence

You and I, alone in the world perhaps, agree exactly on what keeps us grounded – the children's stories! The one you sent along, by Connor age 4, is quite amazing. That the child diagnosed with Asperger syndrome should be able to create this dramatic connection to a friend, to the concept of friendship, the very thing he is usually deprived of because he is unable to express his emotions as articulately as those of others, is astonishing.

And it was, and it was…

Connor – age 4

Once upon a time there was a little old monster which had no friends and no daddies or mums. And he was sad and lonely. Then there was another monster coming behind him. And he thought he was his friend but he wasn't. He blowed fire, he was a dragon. And then a friend came along behind the dragon and the monster doesn't know if it's his friend. And it was, and it was…

Unexpectedly, an autistic child hands us a script, making us all wonder if the label autistic has much meaning when a classroom becomes a theatre in progress.

The Ordinary World

In Chapter 2, I wrote about the hero's journey and how aspects of this universal structure often find their way into the stories that young children dictate. According to Joseph Campbell in his book *The Hero with a Thousand Faces*, the starting point for every story is the ordinary world. This is because we need to understand our hero's circumstances to see what everyday life is like for them before their adventure begins.

Harry Potter lives in a cupboard under the stairs.

Simba, the lion cub, is heir to the throne in the Pride Lands.

Dorothy lives in sleepy Kansas with Aunt Em and Uncle Henry.

As I revisit the stories of three- and four-year-olds I have worked with over the last few years, I realise that for many of them, their first few stories follow in this universal pattern and start in the Ordinary World of their homes.

Jackson – age 4

Daddy.
And my Mummy.
And my brother.
And my Daddy.
And my love.

It took Jackson several months of regularly watching other children engage in Helicopter Stories before he decided to join in. Jackson has communication difficulties, which often result in him becoming frustrated as he tries to get his message across. As time went on Jackson's stories began to include other characters, but this first story was a massive breakthrough, and it made sense that it involved his family.

In a similar vein, Layla's first story paints a clear picture of what life is like in her family, creating an image of a happy child.

Layla – age 3

My Mummy take me to the park.
Make tea.
And Daddy does lots of cuddles and kisses.
My Mummy loves me so much.

Both these stories focus on home and love and the security of a child's world. Although Jackson is not as articulate as Layla, he introduces his audience to the most important people in his world, listing his Daddy twice. But the last line is probably the most important. When Jackson dictated the words, "And my love," he touched both his arms as if hugging himself, and I had the feeling that "my love" was him. I asked Jackson about this, but he didn't reply. During the acting out, Jackson played the Daddy, marching around the stage, but when a boy got up to play "my love," Jackson stopped marching and put his arms around him. Jackson was the Daddy giving love and protection to the child.

The next time I was in the pre-school, I overheard Jackson's Mum talking to him as she settled him in. "Hang your coat up, my love. Have you got your lunch box, my love? Bye, my love, I'll see you later." Although Jackson wasn't able to convey his ordinary world in as clear a way as Layla, he displayed his love for his family through his actions on the stage and in the precision with which he captured the term of endearment his Mum regularly used. In reality, Jackson's Mum referred to everyone as "my love." It was a part of her dialect that she was probably unaware of. But Jackson, who was labelled as a "slow learner," had noticed it, and what is more, he sees himself as the one who is loved.

Fleur – age 4

> The mouse in the house.
> And the mouse played hide and seek.
> And the cat he cooked the dinner.
> And the dog goes make the fire.

The story above shows a different kind of ordinary world. Although the characters are animals, Fleur's story has an equally domesticated starting point. The mouse is the child, while the cat and dog are the parents. Fleur played the cat. During the acting out, the cat and the dog walked around and used their hands to complete all of the tasks as if they were half-human, half-animal. Which does make sense. If a cat is cooking dinner and a dog is making a fire, they will need hands. Still, it is interesting that where usually these children would crawl around when pretending to be cats and dogs, this time, being an animal was less important than the actions they were carrying out. This was a story about family and home. It just so happened that the family in question were animals.

For many of the three-year-olds I work with, this focus on life at home can last for many months. Charlotte was no exception. I shared her two-year-old penguin story in Chapter 2. But when Charlotte turned three, penguins were pushed aside to make room for stories about her family.

Charlotte – age 3

My Mummy wake up.
My Daddy wake up
My Granny wake up
My Grampy wake up.
My cousin wake up.

For many weeks, Charlotte included characters waking up in her stories. This might have had something to do with the acting out and how much fun it became as an activity for both the actors and the audience. Each character took it in turn to lie on the stage and then sit up suddenly with their eyes open. The hilarity this created loses something in translation, but trust me, it is hilarious, particularly if you are three years old. For weeks afterwards, all around the pre-school, children lay on the floor, then sat up quickly and giggled hysterically. Children have a remarkable ability to find the game in everything, and something as mundane as opening your eyes at the start of a day took on a life of its own.

Charlotte's exploration of her family continued throughout my visit to her preschool, with each of her stories mirroring in greater detail the changes going on in her home life. During the two years I worked in her pre-school, Charlotte's Mum and Dad split up. As a result, Granny and Grampy on her father's side, saw less and less of Charlotte. This obviously bothered her, and her grandparents began to feature in her stories.

Charlotte – age 3

My Daddy love Charlotte.
My Granny miss me.
My Daddy love me, lots,
My Grampy wake up.

When acting out the story above, Charlotte took on the role of Daddy. She held hands with the girl pretending to be her and walked around the stage with Granny and Grampy. It was a slower walk than usual, and I wondered if the other children had picked up on Charlotte's sadness. At the end of the story, the children lay down, pretending to sleep, and then quickly sat up, opening their eyes and giggling. Even in a sad story like this, there is still a role for humour.

Having the opportunity to pretend to be Daddy seemed to offer comfort to Charlotte. Through her stories, she tried to make sense of her world and the way it was changing. At barely three years old, Charlotte didn't have the language to explain the sadness she was feeling, but by repeating the phrases, "Daddy loves me" and "Granny misses me," she allowed herself to feel the security of knowing that at least that much hadn't changed. This is another example that demonstrates what stories give to us. When children tell us their stories it can give us an insight into their emotional state.

Throughout the period I worked in her pre-school, Charlotte continued to tell real-life stories from time to time when significant events happened in her life. On three separate occasions, Mum was called away for an overnight work trip. By scribing Charlotte's stories during these times, I was shown how she was processing her Mum's absence.

Trip one – age 3 years and 5 months

My Mummy soon come back.
And my sister said, "What's that?"
Mummy miss me.

Trip two – age 3 years and 8 months

Mummy miss me,
My Mummy go away.
Janie comes to my house.
She look after me.

In both these stories, Charlotte sought to reassure herself. Mummy will be back soon. Mummy misses me. It was as if she needed to hold onto the knowledge that she was missed, and it was only temporary. By telling these stories on these days and taking on the role of her Mummy during the acting out, Charlotte was able to find comfort.

On her Mum's final trip away, Charlotte was nearing her fourth birthday. By now, many of her stories were set in fantasy worlds, and these family-based scenes were featuring less and less.

Trip three – age 3 years and 11 months

It's about Hide and Seek,
And Mummy go away.
The girl can't find the Mummy.
My Mummy miss me.

Hide and Seek is a fantastic metaphor to describe a child waiting for her Mum to return. Setting a missing parent in a game of Hide and Seek is a novel interpretation of what it feels like when someone is gone. That Charlotte can make the creative leap from how she feels about missing her Mum, to what it's like when you can't find someone in a game of Hide and Seek demonstrates her ability for complex thinking. These revelations about how children deal with problems are often missed if we are not regularly scribing their stories and acting them out. Yet, stories like this give us so much information on a child's emotional wellbeing. Charlotte uses story and metaphor to comfort herself, to make her world make sense. This shows emotional intelligence.

Stories set in a child's life aren't always about missing parents. Sometimes they can be about wish fulfilment. Zoe desperately wanted a pet. Her Mum said no. So getting a pet began to feature in Zoe's stories.

Zoe – age 4

Once there was a little pet which was in a shop. And it couldn't get out because nobody was going to buy it. And a little girl said, "That's quite cheap. I might buy it for my home." And she said, "Mummy, look what I've got. I've got a little pet. And it's called Gilbert, Mummy." Then she said, "I think I'll show it to my sisters and brothers. I think my Mum will like it so much. They should buy it for all time."

The dexterity with which a four-year-old tries to manipulate an adult is demonstrated in this story. This is a pester power strategy in action. "That's quite cheap. I might buy it for my home." In weighing up the price and deciding whether or not to buy, Zoe mimics an adult, determining if something is worth the price. In this world, she is in complete control as she tells Mummy that she has bought the pet and is going to show it to her brothers and sisters. In the final bit of her story, Zoe's real-world doubt creeps back as fantasy and reality merge. Zoe really does want a pet. She thinks her Mum will like it, and they should buy it "for all time." You can feel the hope in her words.

In our story-worlds, anything is possible, even the things that the grownups have forbidden. In one of Zoe's stories, a few weeks later, she takes the rabbit home and says to her Mum, "Look, Mum, I have a pet now." In this one sentence, she reaffirms her desire to be in a world where choices like this are in her control. In our stories, we don't need a grownup to make decisions for us. We can do it ourselves. We have the power. We can buy the pet, be given the pet and even get to experience what it feels like to be the pet, and nobody can stop us.

As children become more experienced storytellers, their focus shifts from telling stories located in their home with characters based on their family members. They begin to set their stories in a fantasy world or include characters that differ from those in their everyday lives.

Charlotte – age 3 years 6 months

I'm be a princess.
A dragon help me.
A crown.
And me, Princess.

In the story above, Charlotte tentatively moves into the realm of fantasy. However, it is still something bigger than her, this time a dragon rather than an adult, who helps out. At three and a half, Charlotte is not quite ready to take the lead and needs to be rescued. She also uses her opening line to cast herself. "I'm be the princess." This is something I have seen a lot. It mirrors the way children talk during their fantasy play and how they move effortlessly through a range of roles as they create their theatre. At times the child will be the director, casting themselves and others in their story. "You be the baby kitten, and I'll be the mummy." Next, they become the scriptwriter, adding plot and dialogue. "The baby kitten is sick. Lie on the floor and pretend you are calling for the Mummy. Then I find you." Lastly, when everything else is in place, they slip into the role of the actor. "Poor baby kitty. I'll call the doctor."

Vivian Gussin Paley – Personal Correspondence

Even as the chains around early childhood education grow tighter, more and more teachers are becoming interested in somehow using storytelling and acting to reenact play and the imaginative life in a classroom.

Another Leap Forward

When the children who had been doing Helicopter Stories with me from the age of two or three entered their last term in pre-school, their stories took another leap forward. In the examples below, Fleur is saving knights, Jackson has replaced his real Daddy with a big butterfly Daddy, Matteo is exploring the emotions of sadness and fear through his story of the Big Bad Wolf, and Charlotte is rescued again.

Fleur – age 4

There was a dragon.
And the dragon taked the Princess.
And the Good Knight saved the Princess with a sword.
Then they loved each other.
Then a monster came and taked the Knight away.
Then the Princess saved the Knight.
Then they played together.

Jackson – age 4

It's a big house.
And a little butterfly.
There's a big butterfly coming.
And a daddy one.
And another daddy one.
And another.
And another.

Charlotte – age 4

There was a unicorn.
And there was a dragon.
And a tiny girl walking in the leafs.
She saw the dragon, and the unicorn came to save her.

Matteo – age 4

One day had a secret cave. Then it had a wolf in it.
And had some people coming in the cave.
Then the big bad wolf saw them crying.
Then he said, "What's the matter?"
They told him what was wrong.
They all of them were scared of him.
Then the people were running away.
Then they trip over a stick.
Then the big bad wolf is running as fast as he can.
Then they find a million caves, and they hide in them.

Although these children are no longer telling stories that show the security they find in their family, their stories still involve danger and safety, losing people and finding them again. Even fairytales are about ordinary emotions. Fleur's Princess is stolen by the dragon and rescued by the Good Knight. But when the Good Knight is taken, it's her turn to do the rescuing. As this four-year-old gets ready for Reception, I wonder if she has realised already that sometimes you have to do it all by yourself. Jackson is still a little butterfly in a big house, waiting for Daddy to come home. When it happens, he knows it will be impressive.

Charlotte reminds us of the poetry that is so often present in the stories young children tell. "A tiny girl walking in the leafs," about to be saved by a unicorn. What a vividly striking sentence that creates in the mind of the reader an image of a minuscule person making her way through a gigantic pile of leaves. If the power of language is in its ability to convey meaning, Charlotte, at four years old, has proven she can do this by clearly setting the scene, hinting at the danger and allowing us to fill in the gaps.

Matteo still struggles with his characterisation of the baddie. As a child who is always kind, it's hard to comprehend the notion of evil for evil's sake, so his wolf does the polite thing and asks, "What's the matter?" of the characters he is about to chase. I have seen this happen in other stories, where the baddie is suddenly uncharacteristically polite.

Ollie – age 4

The Stormtroopers were in the spaceship. And the Stormtroopers were shooting the door. And Chewbacca was fighting the Stormtroopers. And Darth Vader was helping Chewbacca fight. And Chewbacca was all in pieces. And the Stormtroopers say, "Sorry."

At the end of Ollie's story, it is as if the rules of the real-world jar with the world of the story, and the storyteller remembers that if you hurt someone, you have to say sorry.

As I look back over the stories of these three- and four-year-olds, I savour my last few weeks with them. Some of them will move to Reception in the primary school I am still working with. But others, including Charlotte, will move to a new school outside of where I work. My knowledge of how her stories develop will cease.

But for all the pre-school children I've worked with over this extended time-scale, I have been privileged to see their language expand and their understanding of narrative move forward in leaps and bounds. It's unthinkable to me that in a world where Helicopter Stories didn't exist, where Vivian Gussin Paley hadn't created this amazing approach, or where I hadn't been invited to work with these children, all of these moments would have been lost, and I would have missed out on the opportunity to learn from them.

These three- and four-year-old children who tentatively came to the stage two years ago are now capable storytellers ready to embrace their next adventure at "Big School." And I will move on too. In the next chapter, I will introduce you to a new group of children that I worked with from Reception to Year Two. But as my time with the three- and four-year-olds winds towards an end, I will leave this group in the safety of knowing that they will continue to battle wolves and rescue knights long after I've stop watching.

Charlotte was the girl I tracked the longest from this group of children. It seems only fair to give the last words to her. This is the story she told me during my last session in her pre-school.

Charlotte – age 4

There was a unicorn. And the dragon came. And it fired the unicorn. And a little girl came to save the unicorn. And there were powers in her hands.

During the acting out, Charlotte played the girl with powers in her hands. She stood on the masking tape stage, her arms shaking as the magic contained in them was released. Charlotte's face shone with the enchantment she'd conjured.

I watched this last story being acted out, feeling a mixture of sadness and joy. I recalled Charlotte's journey over the past two years from Penguin to Super-girl. From creating a character to developing a narrative.

Charlotte was ready to take on the world.

She had grown into a storyteller.

"And there were powers in her hands."

INTRODUCING THE FINAL TROUPE OF STORYTELLERS

From Five to Seven

Actors, writers, storytellers, directors
who took part in the longitudinal study
(in alphabetical order)

Alison, Archie, Benji, Brandon,
Chloe, Daisy, Ethan, Isla,
Lance, Laura, Lia, Liam,
Michael, Noah, Ollie, Patrick.

5 | Crossing the Threshold

"The classroom that does not create its own legends has not traveled beneath the surface to where the living takes place."

Vivian Gussin Paley
(*The Boy who would be a Helicopter*, p. 5)

Original image courtesy of ROH Paul Starr

DOI: 10.4324/9781003161400-6

I've started to see patterns emerging, and they interest me. Having poured over three years' worth of stories told by children moving through Preschool, Reception, Year 1 and Year 2 (aged two to seven years old), I have moments of clarity when I believe I can track the growth of a storyteller and that I am stumbling across some extraordinary theory that will change the way we listen to children forever. Then the moment fades. None of this is quantifiable. The stories children tell are as varied as the children themselves. Some walk sooner than others. Likewise, some children create what we recognise as "complete narratives" quicker than their peers. Each of them is on their own Hero's Journey. I have no intention of creating a guide of ages and stages in storytelling development. Creativity doesn't work like that. Besides, children who hear more stories will have a more expansive vocabulary at an earlier age and a greater knowledge of story structure. However, as I dig deeper, I recognise fragments of a story structure that seem to be intuitively placed in the tales children dictate. This convinces me of how instinctive this stuff is and of the importance of story in our evolution.

Growing Storytellers

The link between language development and the literary skills children gain from listening to a wide range of stories is well documented. However, having worked with children who are fantastic storytellers, even though their story diet is poor, I believe that some of these storytelling skills are inherent. We can teach where to put full stops and capital letters, but the building blocks of storytelling are intuitive. Of course the more stories a child hears the quicker they will be able to use these building blocks in creative ways, but some of this stuff runs deep inside us. How else can we explain the creative imaginings of the child raised in Moscow in the 1920s who grew up without stories, that I write about in Chapter 1?

The two-year-olds I've worked with often tell stories that introduce us to a character. We meet our hero, the penguin, the crocodile, the person eating cake.

As the storyteller grows, they share their Ordinary World, the everyday life of their families and their own experiences. "Mummy, Daddy, Baby."

Around this time, the action starts to appear. The boy is sick, the girl's friend moves away, a dragon helps the princess. These tentative steps into something happening might not come across as full rounded stories, but we connect with the emotions of the character. The boy being sick makes us laugh, the friend moving away is sad, being rescued by a dragon gives us joy.

As our young storytellers become more experienced, they add conflict and resolution. A knight is rescued from a dragon, the people run from the giant, the wolf's head is chopped off, and many of the components we recognise in good storytelling start to appear. Next, I find myself identifying "calls to adventure" and "refusals of the call." Both are aspects of the Hero's Journey. Aspiring novelists study this stuff, and yet this universal structure is present in young children's stories without any training.

Vivian Gussin Paley – Personal Correspondence

Children give dramatic utterance to their thoughts because their thoughts are imagined in dramatic form.

The Call to Adventure

All heroes receive a Call to Adventure, something that spurs them into action. In *Harry Potter*, the call arrives in the shape of Hagrid banging down the door of the hut on the rock and telling Harry that he is a wizard. In *Lord of the Rings*, Gandalf urges Frodo to go on a quest and destroy the Ring. In the film *The Wizard of Oz*, Miss Gulch steals Toto the dog, and to save him, Dorothy is forced to run away.

By the time a child approaches their fifth birthday, most of them intuitively understand that something needs to happen in a story. They would never label it the Call to Adventure, but this move to action, to something out of the ordinary happening, begins to appear.

Daisy – age 4 years and 10 months

There was a little girl, and she was flying in a balloon. And she flew away by herself. And she saw a big bad wolf and a bear. And she runned away.

Daisy told this story in her first term of Reception. Let's examine it using the Hero's Journey. The Ordinary World is the balloon. "And she flew away by herself." The girl accepts her Call to Adventure and is flying away.

Then the story moves to the next stage.

Refusal of the Call

In the second part of Daisy's story, the wolf and the bear represent the danger that lies ahead. They are the antagonist, the baddy. Then the story finishes. Like many stories I've scribed, Daisy reaches an obstacle, and because she doesn't have the tools to imagine a way out, she ends the story abruptly.

This Refusal of the Call is a universal characteristic of story structure. Harry Potter was worried that Hagrid was mistaken and he found it hard to believe that his life would change. This didn't last long. Life at the Dursley's was awful, and he jumped at the opportunity that was given him. However, some heroes want to stay as they are and will only move forward if they are pushed into the path of adventure. At first, Frodo refused to take the Ring out of the Shire and tried to give it back to Gandalf. If it hadn't been for the Dark Riders chasing him, he would never have left. Likewise, although Dorothy initially accepted her call, when she found out that Aunt Em was upset, she gave up the call and headed for home, straight into the path of a tornado.

Imagine if each of these stories had finished there. We would feel cheated. We like watching our heroes experience emotional conflict, to refuse the adventure for a while, but then we need them to Cross the Threshold and embrace the obstacles in their path so we can get on with the story and experience their success. If a hero continues to refuse a call, the story dispatches Dark Riders to chase them out of the Shire, or a Tornado appears to spin them to Oz. The hero must Cross the Threshold, even if it takes an event outside of their control to make this happen. That is the law of storytelling.

This leaves me with a question.

Many of the stories I scribe from children end up with the hero running from danger. If we want our hero to overcome danger, then why do these stories that our children tell, that end so abruptly, appeal so incredibly to their audience? Is it because of the connection that exists between audience and performer? When the wolf and the bear chased the girl in Daisy's story, she squealed with delight at the fear of being caught. Watching her run around the stage, the audience appeared invigorated as if experiencing the danger alongside her. Perhaps the children in the audience are going through their own hero's journey, crossing the threshold into adventure as they watch the stories of their friends being brought to life. Maybe they don't need to be told what happens in order to complete the Hero's Journey because they are completing the story inside their own heads.

Vivian Gussin Paley – Personal Correspondence

Little by little, the notion of storytelling and story acting is spreading around the country. Seldom do I travel somewhere to speak anymore where several teachers in the audience are not actively participating in storytelling and story acting and want to create a network with others, "to make it more fun", as one kindergarten teacher in Boston recently told me.

Amazingly, all roads lead to a most significant characteristic, children quite naturally place their thoughts and actions into story form. Furthermore, they are compelled to act these stories as if on a stage.

To me the nicest thing about what we do is to recognize that the early years, that childhood itself, is all pure theater. This attitude must be and will be the only way to bring play back into the classroom.

Filling in the Gaps

Children are experts at filling in the gaps. When my son Callum was four, he desperately wanted a Buzz Lightyear for Christmas. It was 1996, the year that Buzz Lightyears sold out before they even reached the shops. Not wanting Callum to be disappointed on Christmas Day, I told him in advance that I couldn't get one. Together, we would make a Buzz Lightyear costume instead. I was a single parent and had never made a Buzz Lightyear before. But we got some cardboard boxes, cut a hole in one of them, so it went over his head, and stuck some wings on the back. Callum painted it. It looked pretty awful but Callum's imagination filled in the gaps. Years later, Callum asked about the fantastic Buzz Lightyear costume he had when he was a child. He described it from memory. It had buttons you pushed and wings that popped out, and it made beeping noises when you took off. None of this was true. But in Callum's mind, that was the best costume ever. His imagination created the magic, and the memory stayed with him.

One of the comments I hear most about Helicopter Stories is that children are always engrossed. This is regardless of whether the stories contain a "whole" narrative or a single word. I have seen children enthralled by stories with one character, but how is that possible? How does that satisfy that need for a complete story?

Neurologists have shown us that we connect with the protagonist in a story, but what if, on top of this, when children watch their friends taking on roles, they imagine whole scenarios that aren't featured in the plot?

Many of the characters children see on the taped-out stage they will have explored with the other children during their free play. This is a shared culture of TV programmes, book characters, computer games and make-believe. Although the storyteller might not articulate everything to the scribe, the audience has prior knowledge that enables them to see the bigger picture and imagine the outcome of a story beyond the words of the author. Children are used to making sense of things when they don't have all the facts. Why should story acting be any different? When we watch a programme that ends on a cliffhanger, we enjoy piecing the clues together to work out what will happen next. What if children in the audience are making up narratives in their heads using all the information they have around the theme of the story, and all we see is a small part of this?

In Helicopter Stories, the storyteller's actions often reveal an unspoken aspect of the plot. Maybe they bend down to pick up flowers in the forest, even though they hadn't mentioned flowers during dictation. But what if it is not just the storyteller? A cursory glance around any Helicopter Stories stage, and you will see children in the audience pulling faces or moving their hands as if they too are involved in the action. Jean-Paul Sartre believed that humans perceive things that exist in the world by looking at them in relationship to each other. In other words, we make connections. That is precisely how our mind works around story. We make connections to understand the plot. If things don't make sense; we invent explanations.

Our Amazing Storytelling Brain

Have you ever sat in a cafe next to two people talking so loudly that you can hear every word? Perhaps they're having an argument, and you can't help listening. As you eavesdrop, you are probably making decisions about them. Maybe they're in a relationship. Supposing they're having an affair. By piecing together bits of information, you build up their story. That is our Storytelling Brain, and it often gets me into trouble.

I was in a supermarket a while ago, and I walked past two men. I missed the beginning of their conversation, but I overheard the reply. "I can't even look at PG tips teabags anymore. Not after what my ex did with them." I stopped walking. My storytelling brain shot into overdrive, throwing up solutions that would explain this fragment of conversation. I needed to know what the ex had done with the teabags. Unfortunately, my husband dragged me away before I could hear anymore.

What I went through at that moment links to Robert Dunbar's thoughts on gossip and storytelling. I wanted to examine the story against my code of acceptable behaviour to see where it fitted. Sadly, everything my Storytelling Brain offered is unpublishable.

Until now.

(If the man from Sainsbury's Chippenham is reading, I apologise. Having spent months on this, I realise that teabags are fantastic for tired eyes, but you shouldn't make a cup of tea with them afterwards. Yes, that's what you were talking about. I'm sure of it.)

Heider and Simmel

In the 1940s, two psychologists, Heider and Simmel, created a black-and-white film that they showed to one-hundred-and-twenty people. The film features a large triangle, a small triangle and a circle which interact with each other. The larger triangle repeatedly bumps into the smaller triangle and traps the circle in a corner.

Everyone who watched the film was asked one question:

"What did you see?"

Only three out of one hundred and twenty people gave what would be considered as a logical, plausible answer. Their reply went something like this. "I saw a large triangle, a small triangle and a circle. They were moving around a white background."

The remaining one hundred and seventeen people all interpreted the film as a story. Many believed that the big triangle was a bully, and the smaller triangle was the victim. Some suggested that the circle and the smaller triangle were in love, and the big triangle was a possessive father trying to stop them from seeing each other. Rather than indicating that they had watched shapes moving on a white background, the majority projected character, motivation and plot onto this short animation. The similarities between this experiment and Paul Bloom's modern-day investigation into whether babies recognise goodies and baddies, (that I wrote about in Chapter 2) are apparent, and it wouldn't surprise me if Bloom's initial investigation grew out of Heider and Simmel's ground-breaking work. Bloom's discoveries demonstrate that humans, from as young as three months old, have the ability to endow inanimate objects and puppets with human characteristics and to relate to them as either good characters or bad.

But there was another revelation in Heider and Simmel's work that shone a light on how we create meaning. The psychologists identified that each of the one hundred and seventeen people who took part in the experiment all saw something different. We don't passively absorb story. We play an active role in moulding together all the strands of a narrative into something we understand, and this is possible because of a part of our brain, named by cognitive scientist Kendal Haven as the Neural Story Net.

The Neural Story Net

In his Mediax Seminar, *Your Brain on Story*, Kendal Haven says, "We turn incoming information into story before it reaches our conscious mind." We do this through what scientists have named the Neural Story Net. This is buried deep in our subconscious brain, and it is responsible for processing incoming information in story form. Haven says that what this part of the brain does is that it "distorts incoming information to make it make sense." If the brain can't make sense of something, it won't pay attention to it. Therefore, according to Haven, there is a "make sense mandate" assigned to the Neural Story Net.

> What gets delivered to the conscious mind is a self-created story-based version of the original material, distorted into story form in order to make sense.

Haven goes on to say that if the brain doesn't get all the elements it needs from the source material, it will make them up on its own. This is why two people can hear or see the same thing and translate it in entirely different ways. As listeners, we routinely change factual information that we receive into something totally different, something we can understand. We make assumptions, create new information that wasn't originally there, and ignore whole sections of things that we are told and we are entirely unable to recall them at a later date. On top of this, we infer relationships between two things, we invent motivation to explain why things happen and we layer significance onto everything we encounter. Basically, we ignore the bits that don't make sense and invent things that do, and we don't even realise we are doing it.

As humans, we seek out story. We are the Teller as well as the Told. This is how we make meaning, and it is as relevant to how we consume stories as adults, as it is for the four- and five-year-olds we work with.

Vivian Gussin Paley – Personal Correspondence

I do love the stories you draw out of the children. I'm convinced that no one understands the process better than you do. Your theater training makes all the difference.

Watching you with children in a classroom setting, I saw the natural way in which you made a child feel like an actor in a script, the idea of stage business entered my own practice as a most useful tool, significantly extending the value of the activity as a learning process.

Therefore the child is not only acting out a story, it is developing a professional attitude about the way the role is being performed, a lovely exercise in abstraction and self-control.

Thank you for steadfastly using and expanding the substance and structure of my work, just showing it to be the adaptable and natural curriculum we know it to be.

The Hero in Us All

We are all heroes, choosing to accept or refuse the calls to adventure that life throws at us. Do we take that job? Do we end that relationship? Do we stand up to that bully? However, it's not just in those big life-changing moments that the Call to Adventure arrives. When I first introduce Helicopter Stories to a new group, I invite children to act out stories that I've brought in with me. Then I ask if anyone would like to tell me a story. I think of this request as a Call to Adventure.

As the first child begins to dictate, I am always amazed. They know so little about me, yet they place their trust in my hands. It's incredible how willing most children are to jump across the threshold. Hands shoot up to begin the adventure, even before they know what is being asked. How precious these moments are. How enthusiastically children volunteer, "I'll do that. Let me."

But remember, accepting the call is fragile. Like Dorothy in the Wizard of Oz, it can quickly revert to a refusal if a child's confidence is knocked. When children step over the threshold, we need to be sure they feel valued. I will never forget when three-year-old Rees told his first story after months of refusing. Rees was to play the mummy. He stood up, ready to begin the acting out, and promptly tripped over another child's feet. It was one of the worse things I've ever seen happen during Helicopter Stories, and

I felt so sorry for Rees. His enthusiasm turned to tears, his bravery to fear. He sat on his keyworker's lap for the rest of the session and refused to join in. After that, every time I asked if he wanted to tell a story, Rees shook his head. A connection between hurting himself and acting had been made. It was a month before he risked telling a story again. These moments are precarious.

Rees's story is a one-off. It has never happened before or since, but others also refuse the call, like Lucas, who I write about in the pre-school case study at the end of this book. However, in my experience, they all get there in the end. Somehow, just like Dorothy in Kansas, the tornado spurs them into action. But remember, the tornado is never sent by me. I always keep asking if a child wishes to tell a story, but I will never force them over the line. I don't need to. The momentum of watching the other children telling and acting out their own stories compels even the most reluctant storyteller in the end.

Lance's Call to Adventure

At the start of Reception, Lance was low in confidence, had language delay and was nervous of other children. He was a summer-born child, the youngest in his classroom. Aged four years and two months, he'd never been to Nursery. Standing at the side of the room, Lance watched and listened as the other children engaged in fantasy play. At first, he was uneasy about telling a story, but once he'd begun, he quickly caught up.

Lance – reception (first story)

There was a little girl called Rosie.
And they lived happily ever after.

In Lance's first story, he introduces his sister Rosie. She is the Hero of his Ordinary World. He finishes his tale with a fairytale ending. During the acting out, Lance played Rosie, crawling around the stage, experiencing her viewpoint. For him, this was an enormous step.

When Lance told his second story, he started exactly the same way. This time he included a Call to Adventure.

Lance – reception (second story)

There was a little girl called Rosie.
Then the bad wolf eat her.
Then the end.

Being eaten by a wolf is quite an extreme call to adventure. It could also be called the Final Ordeal. Rosie has crossed the threshold, mainly because it is impossible to refuse a call if you are already in the belly of a wolf. This time the refusal is made by the story-teller. Having set up his scary premise – girl eaten by a wolf – Lance ends his story. In the acting out, Lance played the wolf. He ate Rosie, patted his stomach and licked his lips.

Now, imagine that this story was told from the wolf's viewpoint. It would be similar to when I call my mum, and she insists on telling me what she's had for dinner. It is great for her to savour each mouthful again, but it doesn't really go anywhere. It's gossip. Perhaps the wolf is gossiping about his delicious meal.

Four months later, Lance's confidence had grown. Fuelled by his friendships with other children and the number of stories and rhymes he had heard, the quiet child of September was rapidly become an avid storyteller.

Lance – age 4 years and 6 months

Once upon a time, there was a wolf. Then the little girl said, "Mum, there's a wolf." Then the bear comed to eat her. Then the wolf comed to eat her. Then the mum comed outside. Then the girl said, "No, mum, cos there's a wolf there and a bear there." And the wolf was up the roof.

In this story, the Call to Adventure has been accepted. The girl lives in a house surrounded by a wolf and a bear, and they want to eat her. We have crossed the threshold and are facing the Final Ordeal. The hero has a goal. She needs to persuade the mum to accept the danger. The adult must listen to her as there is a wolf on the roof. Then the story ends.

Vivian Gussin Paley – Personal Correspondence

The intuitive nature of storytelling and story acting has seldom been better explained than during my last visit to you in London.

Twenty local nursery school children were brought by their teacher to a university hall and, with a single sample story became storytellers and actors. They were able to do so with such ease and clarity that the audience of teachers quickly followed the intended design and its connection to play.

"This activity is just like play," one of the teachers decided. "But it is a safer experience. An enclosure, inside of which everyone has the same right to play..."

Cliffhangers and Final Ordeals

Working in the early years can be an endless series of cliffhangers and waiting for the next instalment that may never come. As children's imaginations fire, they happily jump from scenario to scenario, weaving together character and plot, then leaving it to the audience to fill in the gaps as they abruptly end their tale.

As children introduce dramatic action into their stories, these abrupt endings appear more often. Sometimes stories peter out as if the child has reached the peak of scariness they can deal with and doesn't know how to get to the happy ever after. Other times, they jump from the Call to Adventure to the Final Life and Death Ordeal. This is the stage where the hero faces the greatest challenge of all and survives. It's the big fight, the emotional climax, the victorious resurrection. Children often deal with the final ordeal by killing off their characters and then magically making them better. "And then he was alive again."

In the story below, Alison's character survives in a highly creative way.

Alison – age 5

Once upon a time, there was a little girl called Daisy. She was in the woods fetching some berries, and a wolf ate her up. But she didn't taste good, so the wolf spat her out.

Alison wants her character to survive, so the wolf spits Daisy out. When the story was acted, Alison revealed a depth to her thinking that wasn't included in her dictated words. Noah played the wolf. Alison asked him to follow her through the trees. "Pretend I can't see you."

Noah peered out from behind a tree (played by a child) while Alison, taking the role of Daisy, pretended to pick berries. After a while, the wolf jumped out and ate her. As I read the line, "But she didn't taste good," the wolf pulled a face. I gave him time to act out the feeling of eating something unpleasant. Then I read the words, "So the wolf spat her out." Noah pretended to spit, and Alison, who was lying on the floor, jumped up, alive again.

Alison had wanted to show tension before the wolf ate Daisy, but she didn't know how to do this verbally. However, once there were trees and a wolf, she added the tension through her stage directions, "Pretend I can't see you."

Noah hadn't heard the story before, but he showed his ability to think on his feet, respond to the story and improvise. It's spectacular that children do this when they take on a role. They listen to the story intently and respond with actions. This also happens during play; children make up stories, fill in detail, improvise and edit as they go along. It is so sad that these incredible storytelling skills often go unnoticed.

The story below ends up at the Final Ordeal when a boy's house is burned by a dragon.

Ethan – age 5

Once there was a boy called Martin. He went to a house. His house was burnt because there was a big bad dragon. Then someone came into the house. It wasn't a really mean person. It was a nice one. It said, "You're allowed to come into your house if it's burnt because of a big bad dragon. And I will make sure it won't get burnt again."

Ethan resolves the conflict in his story by having a nice person, not a mean one, offering to make sure the problem never happens again. Ethan played the nice person. He spoke with the authority of an adult, reassuring the boy that everything would be okay. Because he likes order and rules, this story offers Ethan the power to put everything right. But the nice person also takes control from the hero. Martin's house burned down, but he never got to fight the dragon because the nice person dealt with everything.

Socrates

Sometimes, as adults, we worry when death or fighting appears in young children's stories. Maybe we don't want to show them a dangerous world. Then, like Ethan's nice person, we shut down the danger before our children have a chance to work through it themselves.

After all, stories are meant to offer an escape, aren't they?

In Ancient Greece, Socrates noticed the irony of this notion. Although stories are places we go to escape, most of what they contain is conflict. The truth is, we don't want our stories to be comfortable places where "nice" people make the danger go away. We want things to be hard for our heroes.

I am going to tell you a story.

Lucy opened her front door. There was a suitcase lying on the mat. Inside were bundles and bundles of fifty-pound notes and a letter.

"Dear finder, this is for you, no strings attached. Enjoy."

Lucy closed the suitcase, picked it up, and walked out of her house. Now she could go on the adventure she had always dreamed of. She didn't pack a bag. She could buy what she needed along the way. Lucy headed for the airport, jumped on the first available flight and flew off around the world. She had a wonderful time.

It's not a very good story. Everything is too easy. Lucy's Call to Adventure was finding the suitcase, but there's no Refusal of the Call, no worries about where the money came from. Lucy crossed the threshold without any struggle. No one chased her to the airport or demanded the money back. It's a happy story for Lucy, but it is so unsatisfying.

Now I want you to imagine a different story. This one is happening to you.

You open your front door. There is a suitcase on the mat, and inside are bundles and bundles of fifty-pound notes and a letter.

"Dear finder, this is for you, no strings attached. Enjoy."

You close the suitcase and pick it up. Now you can go on any adventure. You don't even need to pack a bag, and whatever happens, you will have a wonderful time.

Hopefully, this is more enjoyable now it's happening to you. In stories, we want our characters to be challenged, whereas, in life, we would prefer it if things were easy.

Warnings and Struggles

When we hear something in story form, we don't need time to process it. We experience it immediately, as if it is happening to us. Intense emotions are stimulated, connecting us with the struggles of the main character. Their battles become our battles. Together we learn to fight back.

In his book, *The Uses of Enchantment* (1976), psychologist Bruno Bettelheim said,

This is exactly the message that fairy tales get across to the child in manifold form: that a struggle against severe difficulties in life is unavoidable, is an intricate part of the human experience – but if one does not shy away, but steadfastly meets unexpected and often unjust hardships, one masters all obstacles and at the end emerges victorious.

(Bettelheim, 1976, p. 8)

Likewise, Lisa Cron, in her book *Wired for Story* (2012, p. 9), writes, "Neuroscientists believe the reason our already overloaded brain devotes so much precious time and space to allowing us to get lost in a story, is that without stories we'd be toast."

Because stories stimulate our emotions, we remember the message they contain for longer. This makes them an effective tool for cautioning us about the consequences of our actions. Chloe's story below is a cautionary tale for wolves. To get the full effect, imagine it being told by Mother Wolf, warning her cub of the consequences of eating humans.

Chloe – age 4 years 10 months

> Wolf eat daddy up.
> Wolf eat mummy up.
> Wolf eat grandpa up.
> Rocket land on wolf.

Justice is served.

Often the stories I've scribed that hold the most emotional weight are the ones told from children's own experiences. Towards the end of Reception, Milly told me that she had been caught stealing. She was visibly troubled about it. Then, two weeks later, she dictated the story below.

Milly – age 5

There was a little girl called Alison. She went to the forest. She found a candy shop. She runned to it. She found a big giant candy. She stole it wihout buying it. She didn't share it with anyone. She went into her bedroom and hid under her covers. She fell asleep before eating it all. Daddy found out. He put her on timeout with a big lava monster.

The story has a nightmare quality. The candy is enormous, but rather than hiding it, the girl gets caught because she falls asleep with it in her bedroom. However, the punishment Milly inflicts on the girl is greater than the one she received in real life. Perhaps this comes from a belief that she deserved a harsher penalty. During the acting out, Milly didn't play the girl. She knew that role far too well. She was the lava monster. The audience was about to clap thank you when suddenly, Milly, as the lava monster, pretended to eat up the girl. Milly hadn't mentioned this part in her original story, but it was as if, standing there on the stage, seeing her crime acted out, the monster demanded retribution.

The following story was told by Benji while he was in Year 1. Benji was often in trouble. He rarely got to feature in the Good News Assembly and never won anything. As he dictated his story, I wondered if there was truth behind his tale.

Benji – age 6

There was once a mean alien cat. The mean alien cat got a trophy. He got a silver trophy. More alien cats came to see him.
And then the mean alien cat did horrible things to the other alien cats. They tried to make the mean alien cat say sorry. But he didn't.

Benji's story sums up the unfairness of life. Sometimes the unkind people are the ones who succeed. Even when these people do bad things, they have so much power that they don't need to say sorry. How incredible that a story from a young storyteller can feel like an Aesop's fable for our time. Just look at the people in power today who refuse to say sorry for their mistakes. It isn't fair, whatever age you are.

The final story in this chapter comes from Daisy.

Daisy – age 6

Once upon a time, there was a little girl called Anya. She lived in a house with her mummy and her dog. And they were lonely, and they wanted friends and family. And then they called them and said, "Can you come over to our house because we are lonely?" And when they came over, Anya's mum said that they were allowed to have a sleepover. After the sleepover, they went home in the morning. But Anya and her mum and the cat, they didn't notice that the friends were gone.

This story explores the theme of loneliness. As an only child of a single parent mum with no pets, Daisy often talks about wanting friends to visit her house, but this is the first time she used the word lonely. In the story, Daisy combats loneliness by having a sleepover. The end is peaceful. The guests sneak away, and Daisy, her mum and the cat (which earlier in the story was a dog) don't even notice they have gone.

During the acting out, Daisy played the character, Anya. Another child played Anya's mum, and a third played the cat/dog. We also had some friends and two children making a house around them. Towards the end of the story, Daisy whispered to the friends that they had to leave. "We mustn't see them go," she said urgently. Once the friends left, Anya and her mum sat in their house, stroking their pretend cat. The loneliness vanished. There was something therapeutic in how this story was acted as if the lesson it contained was to be content with your life.

Vivian Gussin Paley – Personal Correspondence

I cannot put our London adventure aside without thanking you again for all your efforts and successes. The days built upon each other, the impression mounted from school to school, culminating in the remarkable conference. And everything connected for me. It is one big story in my mind, and in my Journal, as if all of us took part in the same stage play.

And at the end of the conference a woman came up to me and said, "Something you just told us made it clear to me why I should do the story activity. The outsider, it's all about bringing the outsider in. I get it now."

Where Do Your Ideas Come From?

As I share the stories I have collected over these past three years, I am struck by their depth. If only we could find out what inspired twenty-month-old Anthony to repeat the words "daddy dance" over and over again. Or what instigated Charlotte at two years old to move around like a penguin.

I remembered reading that the question children's fiction writers get asked the most is where do your ideas come from?

One of the best Ted Talks I've ever watched is by Elizabeth Gilbert, author of the novel *Eat, Pray, Love*. During her talk entitled *Your Elusive Creative Genius*, Gilbert tells us that since her book became a best-seller, people have treated her as if she is doomed. "Aren't you afraid that you're going to keep writing for your whole life, and you're never again going to create a book that anybody in the world cares about at all, ever again?"

Gilbert believes that considering creativity to be about success or failure puts immense pressure on artists. When we share a story we have created, we bare our soul. If it comes back covered in red marks, our soul can feel damaged. As a successful novelist, facing, as she puts it, "the knowledge that my greatest success is probably behind me," Gilbert examined the history of the creative process, looking for models that would help her understand this feeling of impending doom.

In Ancient Greece and Ancient Rome, people did not believe that creativity came from humans but instead thought that it came to us from a divine spirit. The Greeks called these Daemons. The Romans called it a Genius. The Genius was a magical entity, similar to a muse, that lived in the walls of an artist's studio. From time to time, the Genius would visit and invisibly help the artist to create their work.

In his book *Common Air*, Lewis Hyde writes, "If we go all the way back to the ancient world… what we find is that men and women are not thought to be authors so much as vessels through which other forces act and speak."

This notion protected the artist from becoming big-headed. If the work was incredible, the Genius was thanked. If the work bombed, it was the Genius who was at fault. During the Renaissance, this changed. Suddenly artists were seen as geniuses. Gilbert believes this led artists to develop huge egos and also to suffer immense pressure.

I love the notion that creativity comes through us and that we don't know when it will show up. When I'm writing, there are times when I'm struggling, and suddenly the answer comes to me, like something external dropping into my brain. Unfortunately, my Genius has a sense of humour. My solutions often arrive when I go to the toilet. I've had many light bulb moments sitting on the loo. Then I have to hold the thought in my head and race as fast as I can back to my laptop.

When children sit beside me to dictate their stories, sometimes I sense that they're not ready. Their Genius hasn't shown up, and they ask to come back later. But other times, their Genius is glowing in their eyes, and the ideas pour out of them.

I asked some five-year-olds where their ideas came from.
Here's what they told me.

Isla We just make them up.
Henry We think about them, and they come.
Isla From right inside my brain. You just have to think.
Benji Cos your brain keeps working and working every day.
Noah When we write stories, we get ideas from those stories to write another one.
Brandon I know stories cause I've had lots of thinking time.
Liam They come from in my head and right down into my tummy and to my feet.
Laura They come from in the sky, in the brain, in the blood and from the pavement.
Daisy A plane gives them you. You know, it flies, like in the air.
Archie My stories come from where dinosaurs live.
Patrick Mine come from dragons.

When the children finished speaking, I found myself wondering if perhaps children's Geniuses were shaped like dragons.

"It sounds like you find stories in a lot of places," I said.

Five-year-old Daisy nodded wisely.

"Stories are everywhere," she replied.

6 The Borrowers

"A day in the life of a classroom is a many textured weaving, a shared literacy, a community of urgent themes. The ancient storyteller seated across the fire under a darkened sky, telling of angry gods and magical omens, creates the same effect, the audience repeating and reinterpreting his stories and adding their own."

Vivian Gussin Paley
(Looking for Magpie: Another Voice in the Classroom)

DOI: 10.4324/9781003161400-7

We are all Borrowers. But rather than borrowing safety pins, matchboxes and everyday objects to repurpose for our own needs like the characters in Mary Norton's novel, we borrow myths and fairytales and fragments of other people's imagination that we recycle into stories of our own.

Borrowing story fragments starts from an early age. A two-year-old waddling like a penguin is soon joined by other children shuffling behind her, and a colony is born. Humans are social beings, and it is always appealing to do the same things as our friends. But I've noticed that the amount of borrowing that takes place inside children's dictated stories start to intensify as they near the age of five. Maybe this is because they have more sources to borrow from, or they notice more details that they want to include. It could even be that by this age, they have more awareness of the relationship between their story and its impact on an audience, and seeing the reactions given to their friends' stories, they borrow bits of them in the hope of a similar response. Whatever the reason, borrowing from other people's stories is a natural thing to do, particularly at the start of your journey to becoming a storyteller.

The Unique Storyteller

We like to think of creativity as unique. When six- or seven-year-olds begin to write their own stories, they are often told to be original. But what does that mean? What is an original idea, and is there such a thing as being truly unique?

In his book, *Mark Twain's Own Autobiography*, that was published in 1924, fourteen years after his death, Twain wrote,

> There is no such thing as a new idea. It is impossible. We simply take a lot of old ideas and put them into a sort of mental kaleidoscope. We give them a turn, and they make new and curious combinations.

This fits with how I see creativity. It's not about producing new ideas. It's about taking fragments of things that inspire us and weaving them together in a way that appeals to us. Even when I've had two children dictate a nearly identical story, one or two of the words are always different. Plus, the intonation each child uses is unique to them. There's no such thing as an original idea. The original part is us and the fragments that the children borrow from each other create a powerful link between the teller and the told.

We are all unique storytellers, blending images together in our own mental kaleido-scope. Children are experts at this. Curious to know what's going on around them, they grab at everything that captures their attention, ready to weave these fragments together into their own stories.

When children engage in Helicopter Stories, they start to see themselves as storytellers, regularly sharing their stories with an audience and receiving immediate feedback from them. For some children, this encourages them to borrow images and topics of conversation that they know to be funny, including these in their stories with the purpose of making everyone laugh.

Gaia – age 5

Once upon a time, there was a little person, and his name was Professor Poopy Pants. And he pooped in his pants every single time. And then he wipes his bum with his hair. Then he called his friends. And his friends were all called Professor Poopy Pants too. And they went home and pooped in their pants.

Pooping in the pants was a much-discussed topic with this group of five-year-olds and Gaia was aware of its power. That was the reason she borrowed it. She giggled as she told her story. The pleasure in the anarchy she was creating was engraved in her smile. Tamara was painting next to her.

"Why doesn't he poop on the toilet instead of in his pants?" she asked.

"I don't want him to. That's my story," said Gaia. "It's a funny one, so everyone will laugh."

"Is that what you want from your story, for everyone to laugh?" I asked.

"Yes," said Gaia.

And to her joy, the borrowed image worked. Everyone laughed.

Other children might borrow a character that one of their friends has already included in their story. By doing so, they share a connection with each other.

"There's a monster in my story today," said five-year-old Milly, to Dylan who always has monsters in his story.

"Is it a bad monster?" asked Dylan.

"Very bad," said Milly.

"Good," said Dylan. "I like bad monsters the best."

Originality doesn't matter when you're five. At that moment, when their story is presented to a live audience of their peers, the author holds the power of the ancient bard. Everyone listens and joins in with something they have created, clapping their achievement. No wonder this activity is so popular.

Helicopter Stories creates communities of storytellers. Like any oral storytelling culture, children borrow ideas from each other to make up stories of their own. Together they discover what works and what doesn't. The bits that stick are revisited again and again, and shared between the group; such is the bond between the teller and the told.

But it's not just the things around us that weave their way into our stories. As I mentioned earlier, our brains have been evolutionarily wired to make sense of the world through story form. Our understanding of how stories work is inherent. We might not be able to articulate it, but we sense the rhythm of a story, the pacing it needs, what we want to happen at the end. When our expectations aren't met, we feel profoundly unsatisfied and may even switch off. The more stories we experience, the more apparent these structures become and the easier it is for us to borrow from them.

We have seen previously how elements of the Hero's Journey are present in young children's stories without them having any awareness of this. But there is another method of categorising narrative that also connects with the types of stories our growing storytellers dictate.

In Christopher Booker's publication *The Seven Basic Plots*, he argues that there are only seven types of stories in the world. According to Booker, there is no unique way of doing stories. Every story can be categorised in one of seven ways. This may sound formulaic, but as humans, we can't get enough of it. When something conforms to one of these seven structures, it is as if the rhythm and the texture of the story connects with some primaeval part of us.

At the start of his publication, Booker compares the epic film *Jaws* with the ancient poem of *Beowulf*, thought to have been composed in the seventh century. *Beowulf* tells the tale of a quiet seaside community whose inhabitants are literally torn apart by the arrival of "a monster of almost supernatural power, who lives in the depth of a nearby lake." Like the film *Jaws*, the ending of *Beowulf* involves a dramatic final battle, the severing of limbs and a lot of threshing about underwater, until the monster is finally slain. The plots of these two stories are strikingly similar. It would be easy to assume that Peter Benchley, the author of *Jaws*, was heavily influenced by *Beowulf*. But that's not true. Benchley never read *Beowulf*. He created *Jaws* from his own imagination.

However, both stories fall into the plot type that Christopher Booker describes as *Overcoming the Monster*. Booker believes that it is this plot type that makes these stories so similar. Rather than Benchley borrowing the idea, he shaped it from a universal story-type that has been in existence since we first started sharing stories.

> When we penetrate to the root of what our impulse to imagine stories is really about, we see there is, in fact, no kind of story, however serious or trivial, which does not spring from the same source: which is not shaped by the same archetypal rules and spun from the same universal language.
>
> (Booker, 2007, pp. 6–7)

Booker identifies the following seven plots types as follows:

Overcoming the Monster
   Definition: The hero overcomes some evil force that is threatening the safety of their community.
   Example: The Three Little Pigs, Jack and the Beanstalk, Dracula, Star Wars.

Rags to Riches
Definition: The poor, downtrodden hero acquires riches or status having overcome adversity.
Example: Cinderella, The Ugly Duckling, Aladdin, The Prince and the Pauper.

The Quest
Definition: The hero, accompanied by friends, sets out to acquire an object of value or to reach a specific location.
Example: The Wizard of Oz, The Lord of the Rings, Watership Down.

Voyage and Return
Definition: The hero goes to a strange land. After overcoming a range of threats, he or she returns home enriched from the experience.
Example: Alice in Wonderland, Goldilocks and the Three Bears, The Lion King.

Comedy
Definition: The hero encounters more and more confusing problems that they attempt to deal with in a way that makes the audience laugh.
Example: Midsummer Night's Dream, Bruce Almighty, Bridget Jones's Diary.

Tragedy
Definition: The hero has a major character flaw that leads to their undoing, and it doesn't end well for them.
Example: Romeo and Juliet, Bonnie and Clyde, The Picture of Dorian Gray.

Rebirth
Definition: The events that happen force our hero to change their ways and become a better human being or transform into something else.
Example: The Frog Prince, A Christmas Carol, Beauty and the Beast.

Once I read about the seven basic plot types, I found that I couldn't stop looking at every story I came across, trying to work out which category it fell under. It wasn't long before my attention turned to the stories that children's dictate.

The Seven Basic Plots, According to Young Storytellers

The majority of stories I scribe for young children fall into the Overcoming the Monster category. There is usually something mean, like a wolf or a dragon chasing them. Many children under the age of seven don't actually overpower the monsters like heroes in more fully rounded versions of these stories do. Instead, they run to safety. Perhaps when most things are bigger than you, and you're told that fighting is wrong, the only option is to escape, or get someone to rescue you. In Sophie's story below, the hero gets revenge, but it's not by her own hand.

Sophie – age 5

A little girl was walking in the forest. A witch was spying on her by the trees because she wanted to catch her and lock her in the tall tower. Then the witch decided to lock her in the tower. "You'll never get out of this tower; it's got a super tough lock. No one will get this lock undone." Then Super Potato comes. And then Super unlock the lock by his super key. And then the little girl was free. Super Potato took them somewhere, which the witch can't find. Then the witch caught both of them, and then all the Super Potatoes rescued them and locked the witch in a new tower. It's tall, tall. And he locked it by his super locking power.

Likewise, in Jenson's Overcoming the Monster story, the evil knight is defeated but not by the hero.

Jenson – age 5

Once upon a time, there was a knight who lived in a castle. And then there was an evil knight, and they fighted. And then a big dragon came and killed the evil knight.

Jenson's battle is won by a big dragon who swoops to the rescue. For Sophie, it's the Super Potatoes who save the day. Perhaps it's hard for young children to imagine themselves as invincible. Is that why their heroes need rescuing? If we can't imagine something, are we able to tell stories about it?

I remember when I was pregnant. I had gone several days past my due date, and I had a recurring dream where people told me I was no longer pregnant. It wasn't a traumatic dream. In my dream world, it was as if there were two states, being pregnant and not being pregnant. Not being pregnant was the same as life before pregnancy, but with the knowledge that I'd done pregnancy.

When I thought about this dream, I wondered if it was happening because I couldn't imagine what having a baby would be like. My dream self struggled to create something it didn't understand. Maybe this is what it is like when you try to imagine overcoming a monster in a world where grown-ups are always saving the day. Now there's a good reason for advocating risky play and for acquainting children with a lot of different stories, so they have a repertoire of heroes and exploits to draw from.

Although many of the stories young storytellers dictate fit the Overcoming the Monster genre, I have seen other genres surface. Several years ago, I found myself scribing hundreds of Voyage and Return stories from a class of Reception children. The start of each story involved the children touching a magic star that took them into a strange world. I still remember how this captured the imagination of the group. Maybe it's borrowed from the Oxford Reading Tree series – The Magic Key.

Michael – age 5

There was a magic star. I touched it, and I fell out my bed. I found a treasure map. You follow the lines, and X was there. And an orange circle was there too. I opened the circle and fell in, and there was treasure.

Stories using the Rebirth plot type involve transformation – the frog becomes the prince, Scrooge becomes the generous benefactor, the Beast becomes the handsome prince. One of my favourite stories within this genre came from five-year-old Shamelia.

Shamelia – age 5

Once upon a time, there was a little caterpillar. The caterpillar went into a cocoon and turned into a butterfly. There was another caterpillar, and it went in the cocoon as well. The two butterflies went into the house. And the butterflies went to get some food from a leaf. Then it flied, and flied, and flied. Then another caterpillar said, "I never, never going into a cocoon." He didn't want to be a butterfly.

The caterpillar's life-cycle is a typical Rebirth story. What I love about Shamelia's version is that it's a textbook opening to the Hero's Journey. The Ordinary World is a place where caterpillars transform into butterflies. As our hero approaches this inevitable moment, she refuses the call. "I never, never going into a cocoon." Vivian Gussin Paley referred to children stories as "novels waiting to emerge." Shamelia's story is a Disney Classic in waiting. In the film version, we would see the various exploits of our character as she tries to avoid the inevitable. It would be a bittersweet coming of age animation about growing up and leaving childhood behind, birth and rebirth. There wouldn't be a dry eye in the house.

Borrowing From Our Friends

Whenever I introduce Helicopter Stories for the first time I start by inviting children to dictate their stories in front of each other. I refer to this as Stage 2 in my book *Princesses, Dragons and Helicopter Stories* and also in MakeBelieve Arts online training programme Helicopter Stories On Demand. During an introduction, everyone hears each story as is it being scribed. Usually, I only take one or two stories across the stage; however, on the rare occasions I scribe more, the depth of borrowing I witness is astounding.

Here are four stories scribed across the stage. The children are four- to five-year-olds from a kindergarten in the USA. I've put in bold the words and phrases that are borrowed.

Liam

Two **pumpkins**.
Three **ghosts**.
Then the **pumpkin flew around in a circle**.
And then the **ghosts** went **around in a circle**.

Kori

Once there was a **butterfly.**
It **flied around in a circle**.
And then there was a bumblebee.
And then the **butterfly hiding behind the tree**.
It crawled and crawled and fell down.

Samantha

There was a **ghost.**
And it was **hiding behind a tree** because there was a monster.
And then it made a trap with **a net.**
And it got **caught**.
Then it got cold, and **it got a blanket**.

Marina

A **butterfly** was **caught in a net**.
And then a **ghost** came,
And a **ghost** found a **pumpkin**.
And a **pumpkin** found a ladybug with a **blanket**.

A quick look at these stories shows us that **ghosts** feature in three of them, and **pumpkins** are mentioned in two. Likewise, **butterflies** appear in two of the four stories. But what interests me is that it wasn't just the characters that were reincorporated; it was their actions. On top of that, all the stories are different. The children weren't replicating whole narratives. They were unconsciously foraging through each other's stories and selecting the bits that appealed to them.

During an introduction, when children tell stories around the stage, each story is acted out prior to the next one being scribed. This means that before they dictated their own story, Kori, Samantha and Marina had seen all the previous stories acted out in the order they were told. They might even have been an actor who brought one of these stories to life. It is this process of either watching a story being acted out or having the opportunity to take part in it that fixes both the narrative and the actions in the children's minds. After this, the elements that excite them most inevitably appear in their own story. If we want children to borrow from each other in this way, this process of acting out and being the audience is vital.

When we look deeper at the borrowing that went on between these stories, we can see the sophistication.

The action of **flying around in a circle** is picked up by the second storyteller, Kori. In his story, the butterfly does the flying rather than the pumpkin. But Kori also introduces another action, **hiding behind a tree**.

Once his story is acted out, Samantha borrows the **hiding behind the tree** action from Kori. She then introduces **a net that catches** the ghost. Cold and trapped, the ghost needs a **blanket**.

In the fourth story, Marina ties everything together. She brings back the **butterfly** from the second story. Catches it in the **net** from the third story. The **ghost** and the **pumpkin** from the first story also reappear, alongside the **blanket** from the third story.

For these children, this is their first encounter with Helicopter Stories. Yet already, they are borrowing from each other and using one story to leapfrog to another, like they do during their fantasy play. This is how story works. Before the invention of writing, it was the only way stories could pass from one person to another – each storyteller borrowing from the last and adding in sprinklings of their own imagination.

But surely there is more to it than the unconscious borrowing of each other's ideas?

Transmitting Memories, Dreams and Ideas To Your Brain

Imagine that you invented a device that can record my memories, my dreams, my ideas, and transmit them to your brain. That would be a game-changing technology, right? But in fact, we already possess this device, and it's called the human communication system and effective storytelling.

This is the start of Neuroscientist Uri Hasson's TED Talk in 2016, as he discusses the findings of his lab in Princeton. By placing volunteers into fMRI scanners, Hassan and his team discovered that identical neurological patterns were formed in every audience member who listened to the same set of pre-recorded stories. This is similar to how heart beats synchronise, as discovered by UCL scientists during the theatre performance at the Savoy that I write about in Chapter 3.

Having seen identical neurological patterns in audiences time and time again, Hassan wondered what was happening in the brain of the storyteller. By scanning a storyteller's brain while they were telling a story, alongside the brains of audience members listening to the story, he discovered that identical neurological patterns are created in both the teller and the told. This revelation demonstrated that the brain patterns formed when we listen to a story are actually transmitted to us directly from the person who is telling it. Our brains mirror what the storyteller's brain is doing. Even more fascinating, if I told you a story, and then you told that same story to someone else, you would transmit to them the identical brain patterns that I have transmitted to you. This would go on, and on, and on, each time the story was passed from one person to another, linking our brains together like a row of telegraph poles.

She Closed the Door With 1,000 Sellotapes

Although no neurological study has been undertaken to show what happens in the brain of young children as they dictate and act out their stories, you only need to look at their engagement to know that those neurons are firing. Where Helicopter Stories happens regularly, we are linking the brains of everyone present in an abundance of shared experiences. This is how communities are born. The children in the examples above began to borrow each other's images after only one session. Imagine what reincorporation is possible with children using this approach over several years. Alongside this, if we share a plethora of stories and poems, there will be no stopping these children in their growth as storytellers.

Having tracked the same children over three years, I was able to observe how sustainable these borrowed images can be. In January 2018, Alison told a story.

Alison – Friday 26 January 2018 (Reception)

There was a little girl called Anna. Her went to her home. Her sawed a wolf. Her run really fast. And then her locked her door with **some sellotape**. Her lived happily ever after.

At the same time, Daisy was sitting next to me, waiting for her turn. She listened attentively.

Daisy – Friday 26 January 2018 (Reception)

A little girl called Belle. And she lived in a house. And she runned away from the Big bad wolf. And little girl Belle had a glass slipper, and she lost it. And she put it in the pond, and it melted. And it cracked at the bottom. And she runned slowly and fast, and fast and fast. And Belle locked the door with some **sellotape** and **Blu Tack**. And some **sticky tape**. And she put it all together. And the prince found her another glass slipper in the pond.

Daisy's story borrows from three sources, Frozen, Cinderella and the Sellotape story that Alison had just invented. But Daisy enhanced this image. Sellotape alone was not enough. She needed Blu Tack and sticky tape to make sure her door locked.

Then comes the benefit of acting these stories. Both Alison and Daisy demonstrated to their class how to use sellotape to barricade a door. It involves much mimed unrolling and sticking of tape to an imaginary door as fast and frantically as you can. In a classroom where children's work isn't shared in this way, this sticky metaphor would have been lost.

Throughout that weekend, Gaia held onto the memory. She'd been in the audience for both Daisy and Alison's story and was desperate to have a go at locking a door with Sellotape. On Monday morning, she begged to be allowed to tell and act out the following story. The class didn't usually do Helicopter Stories on a Monday, but Gaia was eager, and her teacher couldn't refuse.

Gaia – Monday 29 January 2018 (Reception)

There's a girl called Belle, and she was going to the forest. But she saw a big bad wolf. She runned away very fast, but she walked slowly and slowly. She runned faster again, but the big bad wolf quickly ate her. And she was going to her house. **And she put some Sellotape and Blu Tack** . And the big bad wolf crashed the door. He lived happily ever after.

As well as the Sellotape image, Gaia borrowed the speeding up and slowing down actions that had appeared in Daisy's story. During the acting out, she took her time to explore walking slowly and running fast. Unfortunately for Belle, the Sellotape didn't work. This story is more Tragedy than Overcoming the Monster. I wonder if it's because Belle was eaten by the wolf. Maybe that's why her tape didn't stick.

The following Friday, Sellotape appeared in two more stories. This metaphor never appeared in any of the boy's stories. It was solely the property of the girls and it became one of the ways they kept the wolves out.

Gaia – 2 February 2018

There was a girl called Belle. And then she go to the forest. And then she saw a big bad wolf. She ranned away very fast. And then she comed back to the house, quickly. **And then she closed the door, a thousand Sellotapes**. And then she lived happily ever after.

Tamara – 2 February 2018

Once upon a time, there lived a girl called Belle. And she goed to the forest and she found a wolf. She runned and she runned. And then the wolf got her. He putted a cage, and Belle got out of the cage. And she got home. **And she put some Blu Tack and Green Tack on the door**. And she did put on the door a lock. And she eat some porridge and she then goed to sleep in her bed.

The image of a thousand sellotapes is pure poetry. It's also a necessary precaution given how useless the Sellotape was in Gaia's last story. When she finished dictating, she whispered, "Now the wolf won't get in."

Tamara was equally cautious. Uncertain whether Blu Tack and Green Tack would be enough, she added a lock, just in case. Both stories are a mixture of Red Riding Hood and Frozen. Tamara includes a nod to Goldilocks and her porridge. In just one week, from Alison inventing the idea of Sellotaping doors, five stories have borrowed this image. But it didn't end there. Between 26 January 2018 and 24 February 2020, Sellotaping featured in fifteen stories told by five girls, with gaps of several months between each retelling.

Gaia told three more Sellotape stories, two in Reception and one at the start of Year 1. Alison and Tamara told several more stories, both in Year 1 and Year 2. Hannah was late to join in. Her first Sellotape story was in the Summer Term of Reception. After that, she told another one in Year 1 and then another in Year 2. Her last Sellotape story was in February 2020. Then Covid-19 happened, and I never found out if it led to a resurgence.

> ## Hannah – 24 February 2020 (Year 2)
>
> Once upon a time, there lived a princess. She lived in a tall castle. And a witch came, and she took her to her witch village. And the witch put a sweet into the princess's mouth. And then someone came to save her. And then she ran home as quickly as she could. **And then she locked all the doors and put Sellotape all over it**. And then she lived happily ever after.

The gaps in time between each story are fascinating. What is it about an image that enables it to keep coming back time and time again, and with each resurfacing, it's as if it's being invented for the very first time?

The Angel's Cocktail

During his TEDx Talk on the *Magical Science of Storytelling,* David J. P. Phillips, author of *How To Avoid Death By PowerPoint*, discusses why stories linger in our minds. He's named this *The Angel's Cocktail*. When we engage with a story, a cocktail of three hormones is mixed in our brain. It is this that engages us.

Dopamine supports focus, motivation and memory. When our brains are flooded with this, we pay attention to detail. We want to know more. Dopamine compels us to find out the end of a story.

Oxytocin makes us feel human. Referred to as the love hormone, it creates trust, bonding and a sense of generosity. This is where our empathy for a character comes from.

Endorphin is the last ingredient. Increasing our levels of this hormone makes us relaxed, creative and carefree. Too many endorphins and we become over-excited, but just the right amount and we feel wonderfully connected.

I believe that what David J. P. Phillips refers to as *The Angel's Cocktail* is also consumed by children during fantasy play and throughout Helicopter Stories and all other storytelling activities. Sometimes Endorphin levels rise, and as adults, we may become concerned that the child is hyper-excited. But these hormones also explain the focus and motivation possible when children engage in something that fascinates them.

From a Personal, Social and Emotional viewpoint, it also explains how children who engage in Helicopter Stories develop as a community of storytellers. The group I tracked from Reception to Year 2 were highly generous. They enjoyed each other's stories and cared about each other. The Oxytocin they shared on a weekly basis defin-itely contributed towards this.

Dopamine helps us form long-term memories. In January 2018, when Alison and Daisy were acting out the very first Sellotape story, there must have been a lot of Dopamine in the room. This is not the first time I have seen this type of borrowing over several weeks, but the value of working with the same group over several years was that I witnessed how something can resurface again and again, over a longer time frame.

Popular Culture and Gender

Another source that children borrow from is popular culture. Many of their dictated stories are peppered with characters and plots from television, film and computer games. It is these plots that demonstrate the most significant gender differences. Sadly, the cul-tural references of girls and boys tend to be different, even at this age, which means that the sources they borrow from vary. Girls are more likely to be influenced by fairytales or Disney. Many of their stories are set in forests or castles and populated by dragons, princesses, bears and wolves. In contrast, boy's stories are more likely to include super-heroes, Minions, Pokémon monsters, or characters from Lego or Minecraft.

Borrowing from popular culture is often streamlined even further. I have had both boys and girls tell me stories based on the cartoon character Peppa Pig. However, as children start to identify by gender, boy's stories tend to focus on one of the male characters within the tv show – Mr Potato, whereas the girls stories focus on Peppa herself. So even when the cultural references are the same, the way the material is consumed and repurposed often varies.

One of the best things about Helicopter Stories is that although gender differences do appear, we are able to blur these boundaries during the acting out. I have seen girls happily pretending to be the baddy and boys equally enjoying being the princess. Although this gender blurring doesn't filter through into the stories children tell, I have found that children who have been doing Helicopter Stories for a long time are happy to take on any role. Perhaps this is another type of borrowing – becoming a character that we wouldn't usually get to play.

Vivian Gussin Paley – Personal Correspondence

In helping teachers and children become their own acting company, storytelling and story acting creates easily accessible models of linguistic and social cohesion. We embarked upon an open-ended adventure in community building and language acquisition. We learn to listen to one another and take part in each other's stories.

> *How especially wonderful it must be for these children who have difficulty in expressing themselves to see suddenly that the stage belongs to them as well as to their more fluent classmates.*

Slapstick

The stories below were all told by boys. They feature Clumsy Ninja, borrowed from a video game, Minions, from the film *Despicable Me*, the wolf in Little Red Riding Hood, Chewbacca, and some Storm Troopers from *Star Wars*.

Liam – age 5

Once upon a time, there was a little boy called Clumsy Ninja. When he kicked a wall, he fell over and banged his head. And he put a plaster on it. And he lived happily ever after.

Brandon – age 5

Once upon a time, there was a Minion called Stuart. He was riding a motorbike. He fell off and asked another minion, called Kevin, if he wanted to ride the motorbike. Kevin crashed into a tree. And Stuart laughed. Then Bob rode the motorbike, and he crashed into Stuart and Kevin. And Bob laughed.

Sebastian – age 5

Little Red Riding Hood and the big bad wolf throwed her outside. And the big bad wolf throwed her away. And she just fell over. And she got up. And she just fell over again. Then she fell over again.

Ollie – age 5

The dragon was eating the princess. Chewbacca was hitting the dragon. The Stormtroopers were hitting Chewbacca.

Many of the boys I've worked with have a slapstick quality to their stories that I rarely find in stories told by girls. Gaia's Professor Poopy Pants story was an exception. Slapstick produces high levels of endorphins as the storyteller clown punches their own head or falls to the floor in pretend pain to much laughter from the audience. I have seen boys and girls throwing themselves around the stage, making funny faces and having a great time as they act these type of stories.

I have also seen boys get into trouble for being silly when they tell stories like this. I once had an email from a teacher asking how she could discourage this as she didn't approve. I wasn't much help. Comedic stories are as important to the development of a storyteller as stories about Sellotape, or penguins or Mummy. Each form part of a child's exploration of language, pathos and humour. They help children discover the impact of their stories on an audience.

Slapstick borrows from a history of Clowning and Carnival. In the Medieval Feast of Fools, as depicted in Victor Hugo's book *The Hunchback of Notre Dame* for example, the world was turned upside down. Everyone was masked. The beggars dressed as though they were rich and the rich people dressed as paupers. Hierarchies ceased to exist during these festivals, and for a brief moment, everyone was equal. Clowning emerged out of this tradition, playing for laughs, hurting themselves to receive admiration. Many comedians talk about being the class clown during their schooling. There is a power in knowing you can make people laugh, that you have got their attention and are able to provoke a reaction. How wonderful for young children, who are mainly powerless, to have a moment on the stage where they can control the rules. Many boys I've worked with over the years instinctively go for this type of humour. In the tradition of Carnival, they create a world where the rules no longer exist, and it is okay to crash into each other or fall over. For a brief moment on the stage, hierarchies are quashed, and the children take control.

Noah – age 6

Once upon a time, there was a school. And there was lots of people there. And the school was for grown-ups. And the kids went to work. And the grandparents went to the pub.

Previously, I described two-year-olds as the anarchists of the story world, but that title also fits Noah. I remember how he laughed as he pictured the idea of a world turned upside down. Once he had finished, I asked him what the grown-ups were being taught.

"They are learning how to play," he replied.

What better lesson is there?

I often hear a boundless freedom in the children and enormous pleasure in their being able to say whatever they liked and being uninterrupted while they did.

(Carol Fox, 1993, *At The Very Edge Of The Forest*, p. 4)

The Stories We Tell Children

Vivian Gussin Paley's kindergarten classroom was bursting with incredible stories like the *Tinder Box* or the *Twelve Dancing Princesses*. She read books like *Charlotte's Web* and shared myths and legends with her children, alongside making stories up. This rich story diet was a vital part of her children's growth as storytellers. Having spoken about this with Vivian many times and seeing the wide range of sources that the children I worked with borrowed from, I decided to start each session with some poems and a fairytale to see if this would influence the stories they told. It didn't take long before fragments of these began to turn up in the stories children dictated. Many of these stories and poems have been collated by MakeBelieve Arts and are available as part of our online learning on the Helicopter Stories website – www.helicopterstories.co.uk

---

Milly – age 5

Once there was a village full of pasta. Once a little girl came out of the house and found a magic pot. And she opened it. And a monster came out. It jumped in her pond. And it came up to her house. And it messes up everything. And she got sticks, and she banged them together and made a noise. Pah- Pah, Pah- Pah. Pah- Pah. And she killed the monster with a bow and arrow.

The story above was dictated after I'd shared the story of *The Magic Porridge Pot* with Milly's class. Once she's said the first line, Milly leaned forward and whispered, "In my story, it's not porridge." She also added sticks that were banged together, mirroring the different sound effects that I use when I tell my stories. During the acting out, Milly marched around the stage, banging imaginary sticks and shouting "Pah-Pah, Pah-Pah. Pah-Pah" at the top of her voice.

Tyler – age 6

Once upon a time, there was a little old lady with a tall pointy hat. And she was tidying up her house. Then a dragon came and thudded towards her house, And breathed fire onto her house. And then she ran out of her house as quickly as she can. She ran, and then the dragon followed her. And she found another old lady with a tall pointy hat. And then they flew off on their broomsticks. And shot 1000 arrows at the dragon

The first line in Tyler's story is borrowed from one of the poems I regularly share, "A Little Old Lady in a Tall Pointy Hat". The dragon was his own addition, but some of the language he used – "thudded" and "as quickly as she can" – was definitely influenced by the stories I shared.

Tamara's story below is a shortened version of a story that I tell that captured the imagination of several children. For weeks, the three little men appeared in many stories.

Tamara – age 6

Once upon a time, there lived three men called Blue Hat, Gold Hat and Red Hat. Blue Hat and Red Hat lived together. They had a messy house. And one day, Gold Hat came to visit them. He saw that there were crumbs everywhere. He took the little broom to sweep because there were crumbs everywhere. Then the house was all clean. They had some tea and a big bun to share. And they had a sleepover.

Finally, following on from a story that I told about a bear waking up to see snow for the first time and wondering where the colours had gone, Ollie told this story.

Ollie – age 5

There was snow everywhere. Little bear saw the snow everywhere. Squirrel brought a yellow leaf. The fox brought a rainbow drop. A panda brought him some green leaves. Squirrel gave him some berries. Then it was time to decorate the tree. Everything was colourful.

As I leave these five-, six- and seven-year-old storytellers who I have worked with over the past three years, I find myself feeling incredibly sad. I have shared Sellotape and slapstick with all of them. They have made me laugh and taken me to the depth of human emotion.

Helicopter Stories creates a relationship of trust and respect between an adult and a child. Without it, many of these stories and countless others would have been left untold and the experiences of the child that lay behind them would have remained unheard. By having the privilege to scribe children's stories and support them to act these out, I have learned about their feelings, been given a front row seat into their imaginations, and witnessed their gravest concerns. They have shared with me their hopes, their fears, and the wonderful way that they see the world.

Over the years I have known them, each of these children has grown as a storyteller. But growing as a storyteller is a muscle that needs to be exercised and we have to make sure that our children get to experience great stories, to recite poetry and most importantly to play, and play and play, for that is when they uncover the most.

When we prioritise creativity, beautiful stories emerge, and as Ollie says in the story above, everything is colourful.

7 The Impact of Helicopter Stories

Four Case Studies

"Children are born knowing how to put every thought and feeling into story form. If they worry about being lost, they become the parents who search; if angry, they find a hot hippopotamus to impose his will upon the world."

Vivian Gussin Paley
(*The Boy Who Would Be a Helicopter*, p. 4)

DOI: 10.4324/9781003161400-8

The following chapter contains four case studies, two from children I worked with whilst they were in the pre-school classroom and two from children I worked with from Reception to Year 2.

The case studies were created to allow me to share on a deeper level the impact of Helicopter Stories on children who have access to it over a more extended time period.

The two preschool children I introduce you to are polar opposites. Ava rushes forward to tell a story the moment the opportunity arises, but Lucas takes his time to come forward. However, by the time they are ready to start school, they are both highly committed storytellers.

The home life of the second two children is significantly different. Ethan comes from a stable, middle-class family where he is read to regularly. Daisy lives with just her mum in the local housing estate and doesn't have a lot of access to books outside of school. Despite these cultural differences, both children use story to make sense of their world as they take their next steps forward in their growth as storytellers.

Let me introduce you to:

Lucas and the Dinosaurs

Ava the Word Magpie

Ethan the Novelist

Daisy the Girl Who Couldn't Sit Still

Lucas and the Dinosaurs

Lucas wouldn't tell stories. I soon noticed that he refused to do any adult-led, adult-initiated, adult-featuring activity. At three years of age, it was as if Lucas had made up his mind that the things the adults were offering were of no interest to him.

On my second session in Lucas's setting, I asked if he would like to tell me a story. As he turned to run away, I noticed that his arm flinched as if he expected me to grab hold of it and make him take part. My guess is that this had happened to him many times before.

I will never force a child to tell a story or try to persuade or bribe them. I think it is morally wrong. Experience tells me that if I leave it up to them, they will come when they are ready. Lucas's arm was left ungrabbed, and the only thing that followed him was my voice, affirming his right to say no.

"That's okay. You don't have to."

Never Stop Asking

One of the principles of Helicopter Stories is to Never Stop Asking. A day, a week, a month is a long time in the lives of our two-, three-, four- and five-year-olds. It is far too easy to label a young child as too shy, or no good at talking, or anxious about making friends and assume that they will be like it for life because they behave in that way on that day. The good thing about my role – and the fact that I'm not there on a day-to-day basis – is that I see the children through fresh eyes. But even when I'm in their setting over an extended period, I do my best to continue to observe them without any preconceived ideas.

Lucas refused to tell stories, and I refused to stop offering him this opportunity. Each session, I'd casually asked, "Lucas, do you want to tell me a story today?"

At first, Lucas would run to the other side of the room. But gradually, he realised that I had no intention of forcing him to join in, and he'd stop and watch as I scribed a story for someone else.

As a visitor to the pre-school, I was only in the setting once a fortnight. There was no other opportunity to follow up with Lucas or any other child or find out more about them. But during the acting out, I had the most incredible opportunity to learn.

Dinosaurs are the Key

Once I have collected stories, the children sit together around a taped-out stage, ready to act them out. At first, Lucas sat away from the group. As the weeks went on, he shuffled nearer until, eventually, he was ready to join in. It didn't take long to notice that Lucas would only act in a story when dinosaurs were involved.

"Lucas's the dinosaur," three-year-old Charlotte called out whenever Lucas stood up, proving it wasn't just me who had noticed. Lucas shaped his hands into claws and paced around the stage, taking the widest of strides. When the dinosaur in the story was required to eat something, Lucas bent majestically, opening and closing his mouth to chew.

"I loved watching your dinosaur moving around the stage," I said at the end of the acting out. "And the way you bent your head forward to eat the grass. It was brilliant to see." Lucas looked at me. At three years old, he was already checking to ensure that the adults who spoke to him were sincere.

He smiled.

I'd passed the test.

It was the first real contact we'd had.

I thought about Lucas a lot in the weeks that followed, about how important his dinosaurs were. I wondered if this was my way in.

Lucas's First Story

In her book, *The Boy Who Would Be a Helicopter*, Vivian Gussin Paley described the place she scribed stories in her classroom.

> There's a large round table we call the Story Table… here sit the storytellers, picture makers and paper cutters, watching, listening and sounding forth…

Vivian's Story Table was full of paints and glues and lots of paper, so the children could cut and stick and paint while they waited for their turn. In Chippenham, I had a Story Floor rather than a table. The following week I sat on it, surrounded by paper, clipboards and coloured pencils so that the children who were waiting to tell a story could colour and draw until it was their turn.

Finally, the doors to the pre-school were pulled open, and parents and children piled in. The stampede began; names were picked up by parents, who shoved them into their children's hands so they could self-register on the felt noticeboard. Coats were hung up, and packed lunch boxes were placed in the packed lunch box area. Jackson's mum could be heard telling him to "Hang your coat up, my love," and Charlotte was already shuffling her way across the floor on her bottom, pretending to be a mermaid. Hugs and kisses were given, followed by tears. Matteo held tight to his mum, not ready to let go, and Zoe waved goodbye nonchalantly, keen to get started. Usually, this morning ritual would hold my attention as I waited to see which children would join me. Many of them wanted to tell their stories before their parents had even left. But that day, my focus was on Lucas. I watched him walk through the door with his dad, clutching his dinosaur lunch box and skipping into the room. He noticed me watching him and smiled.

"Lucas, would you like to tell me your dinosaur story?" I asked, using the words I'd rehearsed all week. Lucas didn't sit down. He stood beside me, holding his dad's hand while he dictated his first story.

Lucas's first story – age 3

Dinosaur is big and scary.
Dinosaur in a train.
A big volcano.
T-Rex.

"Are you going to be the T-Rex in your story?" I asked when I'd finished scribing Lucas's words. He nodded. "And does the dinosaur go by train to the volcano?" Lucas nodded again. From his nodded replies, I had enough information to help Lucas stage his story.

Celebration

When a child tells their first story, especially as in Lucas's case where they were so reluctant to join in, it is hard not to do a little dance or whoop with joy as those first words leave their mouth. These moments are for us as adults when our most significant acting role must come in. I did my best to be ultra-cool, to pretend that what was happening was perfectly normal, but inside I was punching the air.

For the rest of the morning, I hardly saw Lucas. I was surrounded by the other two-, three- and four-year-olds, desperate to tell their story. When it was time to act all of them out, Lucas eagerly came to the stage. I did his story first, wanting to hold onto his enthusiasm. He sat in front of me while I introduced him to the group.

"This is Lucas's story," I said. I was about to tell them that Lucas would be the dinosaur in his story when Charlotte interrupted me.

"Lucas, are you going to be a dinosaur?"

Lucas's smile was so wide his whole face lit up. "I'm the T-Rex," he replied.

Lucas walked around the stage, taking those familiar giant strides, his hands shaped like claws, becoming the dinosaur we had all grown to love. It was just Lucas on the stage; he was acting alone for the first time, but it didn't seem to bother him. Lucas was a dinosaur, and this was his moment. He growled to show us how scary his dinosaur could be.

When I read the part of the story where the dinosaur was on the train, he happily walked behind the child, whose turn it was as they moved around on their journey to the volcano. This was cooperation we'd not seen before in Lucas, and the Early Years staff and I had to work extra hard not to bring out the fanfare.

The volcano was made by a group of five children. Lucas showed them how he wanted them to explode, their hands flying up and down. Even two-year-old Jessy joined in, waving her arms around with the three- and four-year-olds as if she, too, had realised the significance of this moment. At the end of the story, we clapped.

"That was a good story," said Charlotte, voicing the praise we all felt.

"A very good story," I added. Lucas sat down, the flush in his cheeks revealing that he knew he'd done an excellent job.

More Dinosaurs

After that, Lucas became an eager storyteller. I realised it was best to catch him when he first arrived as, if I missed this opportunity, the pull of the pre-school would be too much for him. When I asked him too late, he'd say no, and then he'd be unhappy when we came to the acting out that he didn't have a story to share. After a couple of hastily scribed stories across the stage at the end of the session, to make sure Lucas felt valued, I decided to make it my job to ask him first thing. It worked, and a flood of dinosaur stories followed.

Lucas's second story – age 3

Dinosaur train came.
And a big T-Rex was making a huge roar.

During the acting out of this story, Lucas insisted on bringing back the volcano even though he had not included it in his dictation. I understood his reasoning. In this new story, Lucas was progressing his narrative from the week before. He was editing in action. So much is going on inside a child's brain when they visualise their stories that it's sometimes hard for them to communicate all of it. This is why the acting is so important. It offers us another layer so we can see their story more completely. In this version of his story, Lucas was focusing on describing the dinosaur, how it was enormous and had a huge roar. This was a continuation of his story from the week before. Therefore the volcano wasn't stated. To him, it was obvious that it was still there. Where else would a dinosaur train go?

Lucas – age 4

A T-Rex eating the meat.
And eating his favourite food with his claws and his teeth.

When Lucas dictated the story above, my clarifying question to help me lead the acting out was to ask him if he wanted one of the children to pretend to be the meat. The idea excited Lucas, and I was greeted by the reply, "Two."

During the acting out, Lucas delicately mimed eating with his claws and chomping with his teeth while two children lay on the floor in front of him and did their best not to giggle.

Lucas – age 4 years and 3 months

A T-Rex.
A Triceratops.
A Stegosaurus.
A dinosaur-us-rex.

For many months, Lucas's stories featured only one dinosaur. Although he allowed children to play other parts, he was reluctant to share the stage with another dinosaur. I saw this in his reaction to one of my questions early on, when I asked whether he would be the only dinosaur or whether there were lots of them. Lucas definitely wanted to be a dinosaur on his own. He was an expert. It was a difficult role for him to share.

I'd been visiting the pre-school for a while when Lucas told the story above. This was his first story involving other dinosaurs. It's a list story, and it did not contain any of the action or drama that Lucas usually included. The difficulty with this type of story is it can look like the child's narrative ability is going backwards. Because there has been movement and description in the past, we may feel a desire to ask the child for more. This is where it is essential we hold our nerve, say nothing, and don't push. If we trust the child, eventually, we'll work out what is going on.

For Lucas, this story was a huge step forward. He was tentatively reaching out to the other children. It was as if he was saying, "I like being a dinosaur, but I'm ready to share this with you."

Four dinosaurs roamed around our stage that day. They didn't interact, just stomped about. Unusually for Lucas, he didn't add any extra stage directions or edits while his story was being performed. It was enough that he was sharing his dinosaurs.

My Final Session

When my time at the pre-school came to an end, Lucas told me his last story.

Lucas – age 4 years and 6 months

A T-Rex.
He's a mean guy, and he's cross.
He bite one of the dinosaurs.

Finally, Lucas was ready to allow others into the action of his story, inviting them to share in the drama with him in role as dinosaurs. Lucas was the cross T-Rex, a mean guy. His face screwed up in pretend rage as the other dinosaurs took to the stage and began to plod around. The biting was done with control. Lucas opened his mouth as wide as he could and pretended to bite at the air.

"The other dinosaurs are cross," he added to his story as it was coming to an end. "They fighted."

The stage was soon full of pretend dinosaurs pretending to fight. Lucas's eyes shone. Finally, he was connecting with the other children, and he enjoyed what they added to his story. As I left that day for the last time, I overheard Lucas saying to one of his friends.

"I'm the T-Rex, and you're the Stegosaurus, and we're looking for something to eat."

He didn't say goodbye to me.

Dinosaurs are too busy for sentimental stuff like that.

Ava the Word Magpie

In most classrooms I visit, there is at least one child who demonstrates such great aptitude for playing with words that it captivates my heart. These are the Word Magpies, the children who insert into their stories odd phrases or expressions that they have heard before, savouring each sentence as if they can taste the goodness inside. Language is poetry to these children. They dictate their stories with calm precision, searching for the correct phrase in that catalogue of words that exists in their brain. The moment these children speak, without knowing anything about them, I can tell that their homes contain an abundance of made-up stories and that they are read to regularly. These children have a head start in life.

Ava, aged four, was one such child. Her peers are the children you have already met, Lucas and Jackson, Zoe and Charlotte, Matteo and Harper. Her pre-school is in one of the poorest areas of Wiltshire. Her parents are not wealthy, but here is a child who is read to, engaged in conversation and listened to. That is where her riches come from.

Ava arrived at the pre-school at the start of my second year of working there. There were several new children that term, and I was doing an introduction to Helicopter Stories for those who didn't know it already. I noticed her straight away. I had asked for a volunteer to tell a story across the stage when her hand shot up. Confident and trusting, she was ready to take the risk of telling a story to a stranger

Of course, that in itself is not unusual. Lots of hands shot up around the stage that day. They always do. I am staggered by how willing young children are to take such a risk, to put up their hand to tell a story or share something they are thinking and trust that the adult will value it. How important it is, after such a display of faith, that we don't undermine their contribution. As we grow older, this simple act of putting ourselves forward is much harder to do, maybe because we've learned that we're not always listened to, or we're frightened of getting something wrong. When I've run face-to-face training with adults, I can sense the anxiety in the room when they realise I need one of them to tell me a story. We must make sure we don't betray children in this way. I love going to the theatre, but shows that invite children onto the stage so actors can make fun of them for the audience's amusement is one of the clearest examples I have of this type of betrayal. How can we be creative when we don't feel secure? Security comes from not being judged.

Thankfully, Ava knew she was in safe hands. She shuffled across the stage, and we sat side by side, her dictating, me scribing, working together to demonstrate how story dictation works.

Ava's first story – age 4 years and 3 months

Once upon a time, there was a little girl called Little Red Riding Hood. And her mum says, "Can you go to the Granny person?" And the wolf saw her. And the wolf got there first. And the wolf ate the Granny person up by one gulp.

Ava spoke slowly, staring into space as if picturing her story on an invisible screen a few feet in front of her. I have seen other children do this. It's as if they are projecting their imagination at a fixed point in space and are dictating what they see. Her voice was hypnotic, drawing us in. She meticulously selected each phrase and then watched intently as I scribed her words on the page. When we acted Ava's story, she played Red Riding Hood. As she skipped around the stage, she stopped every now and then to pick up an imaginary flower. She was so engrossed in this acting that she didn't notice Matteo, who was playing the wolf, and his fabulous movements as he ate up Grandma.

When I looked back at Ava's first story, I noticed that the mother's dialogue was full of character. "Can you go to the granny person?" The way she delivered this line, with her emphasis on the word person, gave the impression of an adult explaining a difficult concept to a child. This Granny was a person, not an animal or an object. I was also struck by the clarity of detail contained in this story, particularly around the sequence of events.

"And the wolf saw her.

And the wolf got there first.

And the wolf ate the Granny person up by one gulp."

These last three sentences are from the wolf's viewpoint, not Little Red Riding Hood's. The wolf is the central character, and the timeline of the events is from his perspective. The wolf sees Red. He gets there first. He eats Granny. Often young storytellers get confused with sequencing. They jump tenses or muddle up the order that things happen. But Ava spoke in a precise way. Through her repetition of the phrase "And the wolf…" she sets up a rhythm to her story that draws us in. She uses this phrase three times. The rule of three is a principle that runs through some of our greatest stories, fairy tales and myths. There is a reason for this. Three is the smallest number of components needed to create a pattern. As humans, our brains seek out patterns. We can't get enough of them. They make content more memorable and are profoundly satisfying to us on a deeper level. The repetition of "And the wolf…" is not a phrase Ava has borrowed from a story. She created it, demonstrating how inbuilt this structure is for children who hear stories regularly.

Filling in the Detail

The following week, Ava continued to work on her Little Red Riding Hood story, allowing herself some time to fill in the detail. This process of editing a story from the week before, without any prompting from an adult, is something that I have seen happen a lot with Helicopter Stories. There is an excitement for young children in revisiting moments that are memorable. Some children do this by using almost exactly the same words week after week. The joy for them is in the memory of how it was acted out, and by telling the same story, they get this to happen again and again. Others, like Ava, and Lucas in the previous case study, use this opportunity to make changes to their script or fill in the detail, like writers developing their ideas.

I have had several teachers contact me about children who continue to tell the same story. They wonder how to move a child on to a new topic. Children will move on when they are ready. As a writer myself, I relate to this process of revisiting the same story or the same piece of text over and over again. My first draft is about getting the outline down. The second is where I hone what I am saying, keeping the bits I like and discarding the rest. But even if you don't consider yourself a writer, there are things that fascinate you, that you enjoy. These are the areas that take our focus, where we develop our expertise. Children are no different. Ava used her second story to fill out the details from the week before, adding in a character description and more emotional content.

Ava's second story – age 4 years and 3 months

Once there was a Little Red Riding Hood. Her mum said, "Go to the Granny person." Then she putted her red cloak on and her red hood on. Then she went outside to go to the Granny person. Then a wolf saw her. And he got to her and eated her up by one gulp. Then she screamed. And her dad was nearby and heard her. And he chopped the wolf's head off.

This revised version was from Red Riding Hood's viewpoint, and the audience experienced the panic in her scream. It was a blood curdling, no-holds-barred type of scream. Ava shared it with us loudly during the acting out. Although the "Granny person" is still here, she's a mere cameo role, the impetus for Red Riding Hood's journey, but that is all. She doesn't even get eaten, and Charlotte, who played her, had to wait in her house while all the action took place outside. Having taken part in the session the week before, Ava was familiar with how Helicopter Stories worked, so she gave the character Red Riding Hood more of a starring role. Before Red Riding Hood arrives at Granny's, she is eaten up "by one gulp." Thankfully, Red Riding Hood does not remain eaten for long. Following that impressive scream, Dad chops the wolf's head off, and all is well with the world.

Storytelling allows children to face monsters, to be eaten up "by one gulp," to "die" briefly. Children know this is only pretend. Capture is often followed by a swift rescue. The Daddy or the Woodcutter saves Little Red Riding Hood, the one who dies is alive again, and that which is wrong is put right. That's unless you're the wolf, of course, and someone cuts off your head, but then baddies aren't meant to survive.

A friend of mine shared a story they had heard about a girl who had been told a version of Red Riding Hood where the wolf ran away and was still out there somewhere. The child was having nightmares about a wolf coming to get her. Eventually, following advice, the parents retold the story, but this time they used the version where the Woodcutter cuts open the wolf's tummy and filled it with stones. The wolf drowned in the river. This might be a gruesome way to die, but the girl loved it. Her nightmares stopped. She knew the wolf had been dealt with. Her parents may have initially hoped to pass on a lesson about forgiveness by setting the wolf free, or perhaps they were concerned that a more violent version wasn't appropriate for their child. But fairy stories reach into a deeper part of our unconscious and are a safe place to act out revenge.

Painting Pictures with Words

Over the following weeks, Ava regularly told stories and grew more specific in her choice of words as she painted the pictures of her scenes.

Ava – age 4 years and 4 months

Once there was a little lady who was trying to get her children to look after the Dad. A dinosaur came into the house. And then a tree was outside, And the wind blew the tree down. And then another dinosaur come into the house. And then the children got rid of the animals. And they cleared them out of the house.

This story is not based on one that I know, and my assumption is that Ava made it up. It has all the ingredients of a fully rounded story. The children are tasked with looking after Dad, and things start to go wrong. Even Ava's phrasing of the first line is unusual. "Once there was a little lady who was trying to get her children to look after the dad." This concept of trying is very sophisticated and shows an awareness of how difficult this might be from another character's viewpoint. The little lady was not just telling the children to do something but trying to persuade them to do it. She might not be successful. Thankfully the chaos caused by the dinosaurs and the falling tree is eventually put right. The children clear everything up and save the day.

As Ava starts inventing her own stories, she demonstrates her understanding of how narrative works. In a few short words, making it up as she goes along, without any planning or preparation, Ava outlines a plot with recognisable characters, a conflict and a resolution.

Ava – age 4 years and 5 months

One day a little girl was picking some flowers. She go ask her mum if she could borrow the flowers in her collection. With all her might, a bird go and pick one bit of her collection. Then her mum said, "Look little darling, a bird go and pick some of my collection."

When Ava told this story, I had the feeling she was savouring the word "collection" in her mouth. For me, this story is a celebration of words, of how they feel when you speak them, of the way they shape your lips. Ava repeated the word "collection," three times, each time pronouncing every one of the three syllables. She also modelled her knowledge of story language and her ability to magpie words. "With all her might," is a fairytale phrase, and "Look little darling" is something a mother might say to a child.

Children imitate the language they hear. The more they are read to, spoken to, conversed with, the more words are available for them to try out. Ava's early childhood was surrounded with rich language. Sometimes, when she spoke, it was like she was remembering a fragment of a story she had heard long ago. Other times, she would become much more focused and it was as if her imagination was being projected onto a screen, and all she had to do was dictate what she saw.

Moving into Reception

As Ava neared the end of her time in pre-school, she told me a story about a dinosaur and a snake.

Ava – age 4 years and 6 months

A person says, "Watch out unicorn there's a dinosaur and a snake." And then a neighbour says, "Don't worry, I'm rescuing the unicorn." And then the snake slithers onto the tree. And the dinosaur climbs onto the tree. And that was the one that the neighbour chased them up.

After this story, I didn't get to see Ava for around five months. By the time I did, she was four years and eleven months and had moved to Reception. On my first day in her reception classroom, Ava told me the following story. Bearing in mind the length of time that had passed, I couldn't help but be struck by the similarities between the two stories.

Ava – age 4 years and 11 months

Once upon a time, there was an old lady living with an old, old, old man in an old, old, old house. One day a dinosaur and a snake and all nasty stuff came. And then another day, in a tree, a man was there with a rope that was going to take those nasty animals away. And then the house turned into a beautiful palace. And then they went in their car, and their car turned into a coach. And then the one that saved them turned into the driver of the coach.

The dinosaur, the snake and the tree all make their return in this sequel to her preschool story. But again, we see Ava editing and adapting, even after five months have passed. Dinosaurs and snakes cause trouble, but because of the tree, they are saved, and a man is able to take the animals away. A fairy-tale theme emerges where the people who are saved are transformed into royalty, cars are changed into coaches, and even the rescuer is given the role of driving the coach. Story language is again a feature in Ava's story. The repetition of "old, old, old" is one that is used to great effect in storytelling to add emphasis to a word. This type of repetition often comes in groups of three, exactly as Ava demonstrates.

Ava's love of words enables her to revisit her stories even after time has passed. Her engagement with language and imagery enriches her stories with a sophisticated feel. All these examples are before she even reaches the age of five. If we need evidence of the value of sharing stories with children, Ava and many children like her are the proof. How sad it is that not all children have access to this gift. Imagine what our classrooms would look like if greater numbers of children had the opportunity to engage with stories routinely from the time they were born. Just think what would happen to their stories.

Ethan the Novelist

"When I grow up, I'm going to write a book," said five-year-old Ethan. "I've started already, but when I'm grown up, it will get bigger. I love writing stories." Ethan was one of the oldest in his class. From an academic perspective, he was also the highest achiever. In October of Reception, while most other children had just started mark-making, Ethan was already writing legible stories and having a go at complex spelling. Once, when I asked him if his family did bedtime stories, he told me that his Dad was currently reading him *The Hobbit*.

Ethan's first self-written story was created within days of him being introduced to Helicopter Stories. After that, there was no stopping him. If it wasn't his turn to dictate (and often as an additional story on the days when it was his turn), Ethan would sit at a table, pen in hand, turning out page after page of writing. Before I share examples of stories written by this incredibly literate five-year-old, I want to show two of the stories that Ethan dictated during his first term in Reception. This will give you an idea of his language development and the themes contained in his stories.

Ethan – age 4 years and 11 months

Once there was a really, really big, mean dragon and he was hungry, so he decided to catch some children. But all he find was a little flower. So he walked around some mountains, but there were no children to be seen. Then he walked around the jungle. Then finally he found some children. Then finally, he gobbled them all up. And then he lived happily ever after.

Throughout this story, Ethan sticks with the viewpoint of the big, mean dragon, who is the main character. This creates a clear line through the narrative, which makes the story deeply satisfying. The dragon is an anti-hero, the type of character who is not supposed to be liked but that we root for anyway. As readers, we generally don't want our heroes to gobble up children. Still, there is something compelling about a hero who sets out to find food and instead finds a flower. The dragon then ends up on a journey across mountains and jungles until he finally finds what he is looking for and gobbles it up.

It is rare that I have scribed a quest story for a child under the age of seven. Most young children favour the Overcoming the Monster plot type. But Ethan's story is a Quest. If we substitute the word "children" with the word "chalice," and instead of eating them, the dragon wants to own them, we have a story that falls within the quest format. The hero sets off on a journey to a far-off place in order to uncover an object or achieve a goal. Of course, it makes sense that Ethan is already starting to use this more complex plot format. We know that he is already listening to quest type stories like *The Hobbit*. Plus, we can see by the words he uses that he has the language capacity of a much older child. There is also satirical humour contained in his story. Again, it breaks the rules. We meet a hero we wouldn't usually like, presented in a way that makes us root for him.

During the acting out, Ethan-the-dragon tiptoed off on his adventure. Other children used their bodies to become the vines in the jungle, the mountain that the dragon walked around and the flower he found at the start. As Ethan-the-dragon approached the child playing the flower, he took a big sniff as if hoping it was something to eat. Then he sighed, shook his head and set off around the mountain. Through these actions, Ethan added another layer to the original story. He gave the character purpose.

As I reread the dictated story below, I wondered if Ethan was sharing with his audience, albeit unconsciously, how he sees the world.

Ethan – age 5 years and 1 month

There was a little girl called Belle. She went to the palace. And in the palace, she saw a big, bad wolf. "Get out of here. It's not your home. It's mine," said the wolf. "Find somewhere else to live," he said. But the girl was puzzled. She wanted her house back. And the wolf said, "Okay, as long as you give me as many strawberries as you can." "Okay," said the princess in a whining voice.

I often thought it was hard for Ethan. Academically, he was miles ahead of the rest of the children, but he struggled to fit in socially. Finally, Helicopter Stories gave him that place. Here, everyone is equal. It's the great leveller. Every story is valued without judgement, and there is no right or wrong. Plus, during the acting out, Ethan was able to play with others without being excluded. Everyone took part in his stories without him having to ask them. It was like having a lot of friends. On top of this, he got to act in stories told by children who had never been read to and who didn't have the same rich language background as him. Children he would never usually play with. All of those barriers were broken.

After I'd worked in Ethan's classroom for a few months, his Mum sent me an email, thanking me for helping her son find his place. She told me that the stories were helping him, and he'd found such a passion for them. Perhaps Ethan was like the princess in the story above, believing he was in his own home, but puzzled about why he didn't fit. What if the strawberries in that story are metaphors for the stories he loves telling, perhaps he has to keep telling them to ensure he is always welcome? The best thing about Helicopter Stories is that it appreciates all children. As Ethan's class grew in empathy and emotional intelligence, Ethan began to make friends.

In both of Ethan's dictated stories above, his wry sense of humour shines through. Interestingly, both focus on the villain, the big bad wolf, the mean dragon, the one that doesn't fit. These anti-heroes feature a lot in Ethan's stories as if he's exploring the relationship between good and bad, between being wanted and not belonging. Alongside this, his dictated stories reveal the precision of his language, his use of words like "puzzled" and "whining," the way he includes dialogue in his stories. Ethan has experienced a vast range of stories and has many sources to draw from.

Throughout Reception, Year 1 and Year 2, Ethan grew into a prolific storyteller and writer. It would be easy to celebrate his quick jump to writing, as if we have succeeded in our goal, and we no longer need to scribe for him. But the stories Ethan wrote by himself in those early days lacked the rich language of the ones he dictated. So although it is incredible that he created them, I was delighted when his teachers agreed with me that we needed to keep scribing for him, alongside encouraging his own writing.

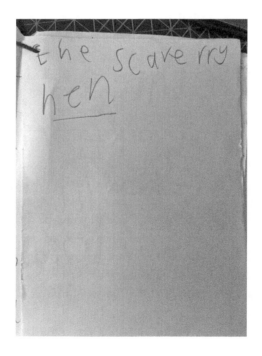

Fig 1

Fig 2

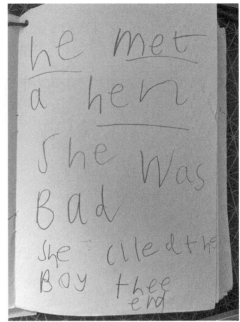

Fig 2a

Transcription:

Ethan – age 4 years and 11 months

The Scary Hen.
Once there was a boy called Leo. He met a hen. She was bad. She killed the boy. The End.

To write this story, Ethan created a book by folding a sheet of A4 in half and giving it a title. He also had a go at spelling the word scary, which isn't easy phonetically. This is a child who has just celebrated his fifth birthday.

The story features an anti-hero who wins in the end. The hen is bad; she kills the boy. This is the same type of humour we have seen earlier in Ethan's dictated stories, but the richness of his language is lost in his effort to write. As a result, Ethan has shortened his story dramatically. However, it is still an impressive story. It is complete. It has a beginning, a middle and an end. It also fits within the tragedy structure that was demonstrated in the seven basic plots model.

From this first self-written story on a folded piece of A4, Ethan began to make the connection between the stories he wrote and the books he read. He became a novelist. From then onwards, there was no stopping him.

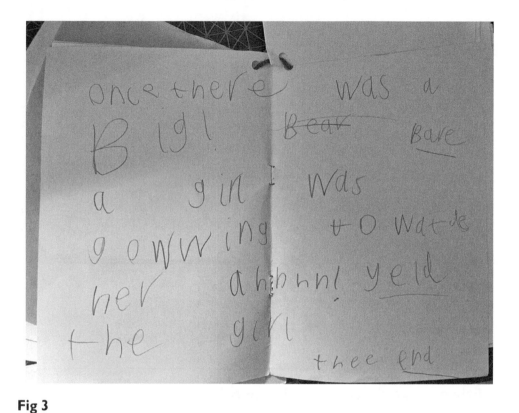

Fig 3

Transcription:

Ethan – age 5

Once there was a big bear. A girl was going towards her. "Ahhhhh!" yelled the girl. The End.

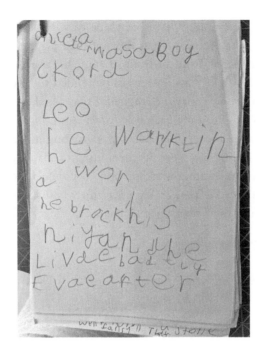

Fig 4

Transcription:

Ethan – age 5 years and 1 month

Once there was a boy called Leo. He walked into a wall. He broked his knee. And lived badly ever after.

Ethan's stories still make me laugh. The ones he wrote during that year in Reception are like an abbreviated version of his dictated stories. They are jokes in story form, often resulting in something bad happening to the hero. Ethan challenges the notion of happy ever after. His tragicomedy stories end miserably for both the boy who walked into a wall and the girl who walked over to a bear. Through both his writing and his dictating, Ethan has found a place to be subversive. In the carnivalesque way I discussed in the previous chapter, he reverses the power structure for his characters. Baddies win. People get hurt and don't get better. Unfortunately, in Ethan's tragicomedies, it never ends well for our hero.

But there was more to it than just the cleverness of Ethan's writing. Because the stories were acted out, Ethan was given a chance to share his type of humour with the class in a way that he wouldn't have been able to without Helicopter Stories. For example, when acting out the bear story above, Ethan played the bear. He stumbled towards the girl, his arms held out in front of him, his mouth open and a comedic look on his face. As the child playing the girl pretended to scream, Ethan did a little dance and rubbed his tummy. Everyone laughed. Ethan liked the power of these flawed characters, but he also liked to milk each role for the humour.

By March of his year in Reception, Ethan was growing more confident as a writer. Many of the children in his class were just beginning to shape letters, so Ethan would scribe for them. This was another way for him to connect, to celebrate his gift by helping others. Sometimes I'd send children to him when they wanted to write their own story, and it was not their turn to be scribed.

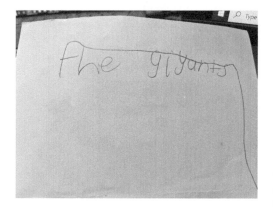

Fig 5

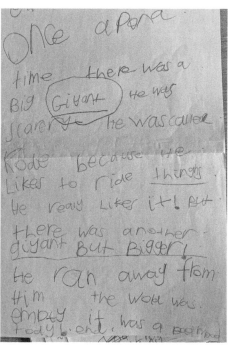

Fig 5a

Transcription:

Ethan – age 5 years and 4 months

The Giants
Once upon a time, there was a big giant. He was scary. He was called Rode because he likes to ride things. He really likes it! But there was another giant. But bigger. He ran away from him. The world was empty. It was a bad mood day.

The story above is already beginning to look more like the stories that Ethan scribed. His quirky humour is ever-present. The wordplay used to name the giant is true to Ethan's idea of clever fun. Of course, the giant is called Rode because he likes to ride. What other name could there be for him? Ethan's humour was often lost on the others in his class. Still, the adults found it funny, and Ethan was used to playing to an older audience.

When Ethan came to the end of the acting out for this story, he stood alone on the stage, looking around him at the empty world. Then a thought struck him.

"I don't think the giant should have run away from the other giant," he said. "Now, he's got no one to play with." Ethan sat back in the audience. I could tell he was still thinking about it and trying to work out the implications.

Ethan continued to dictate and write his own stories throughout Reception Year 1 and until the Spring Term of Year 2. His commitment never stopped. Nor did his portrayal of characters who didn't quite fit. Below are the last two stories he wrote before the Covid-19 lockdown meant I stopped working in his classroom.

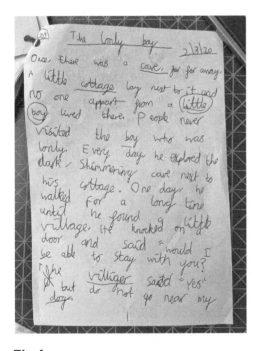

Fig 6

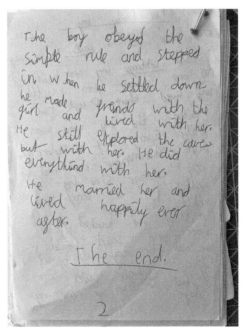

Fig 6a

Ethan – age 7 (Year 2)

Once there was a cave, far, far away. A little cottage lay next to it. And no one apart from a little boy lived there. People never visited the boy who was lonely. Every day he explored the dark, shimmering cave next to his cottage. One day he walked for a long time until he found a little village. He knocked on a door and said, "Would I be able to stay with you? The villager said, "Yes, but do not go near my dog." The boy obeyed the simple rule and stepped in. When he settled down, he made friends with the girl and lived with her. He did everything with her. He married her and lived happily ever after.

As I read this story, I smiled. No longer the anti-hero, Ethan was now able to embrace the true hero within himself. Here is a lonely boy who set out on his own hero's journey to find companionship. He has learned to obey the simple rules, and as a result, has found happiness.

The story below was scribed on the same day. Within a one and a half-hour session, Ethan scribed two stories. This prolific writer truly has the makings of a novelist.

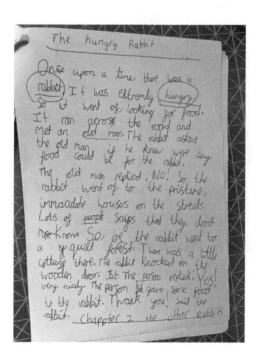

Fig 7

Ethan – age 7 (Year 2)

The Hungry Rabbit
Once upon a time, there was a rabbit. It was extremely hungry, so it went off, looking for food. It ran across the road and met an old man. The rabbit asked the old man if he knew where any food could be for the rabbit. The old man replied, "No!" So the rabbit went off to the pristine, immaculate houses on the streets. Lots of people says that they don't know. So, off the rabbit went to a quiet forest. There was a little cottage there. The rabbit knocked on the wooden door. The person replied, "Yes!" very nicely. The person gave some food to the rabbit. "Thank you!" said the rabbit.
Chapter 2 : The Other Rabbits

I never did get to find out what happened when the rabbit hero met the other rabbits. Covid-19 stopped me from visiting Ethan's classroom. I hope they made friends, and the hungry rabbit found a place where it would fit. Ethan found his way to connect with his classroom through story. Maybe the hungry rabbit will do likewise.

One thing I do know is that Ethan will be okay. He is already writing chapter books at the age of seven, creating story arcs, resolutions, and filling page after page with his quirky humour and complex thinking beyond his years.

"When I grow up, I'm going to write a book," said five-year-old Ethan.

"You certainly are," I replied.

Daisy the Girl Who Couldn't Sit Still

Daisy never stopped moving. Her head turned from side to side, and her eyes looked up and down, and back and forth, and all around the room, anxious not to miss anything.

Daisy never stopped talking. There was always something to comment on, to notice, to share, to tell the room for fear that if she didn't say it out loud, that wonderful thought that had just popped into her mind would vanish forever.

I like your necklace. Are they new shoes? Ooh, can I have some paper? Tamara's spilt her drink on the carpet. That's my picture up there on the wall. Why is Benji sitting on that chair?

Daisy provided a running commentary of life in the Reception classroom. She saw everything, stated everything, and knew everything that was going on. When the children were required to sit on the carpet, Daisy would always be the last to sit down, just because she could. Then she'd pretend that she hadn't realised what was expected of her. Of course, her smile gave her away, and she was always getting into trouble.

Daisy was difficult, disruptive, distracting.

She reminded me of me.

Daisy's home had very few books, and she rarely heard a bedtime story. She was growing up in a single-parent family and had no contact with her dad. But it was not just these cultural similarities that connected us. Daisy's ability to get into trouble for chattering continually, her need to tell stories about everything she saw, her inability to sit still and how frustrating this was for the adults that taught her all reminded me of my time in school. Like me, Daisy was a kinaesthetic learner. She needed to move to think. This is often difficult in a classroom. Over the three years that I scribed stories for Daisy, I watched in fascination at her growth as a storyteller, wondering if access to Helicopter Stories would help her to find a belief in herself that my schooling had denied me.

Being part of the community was vital to Daisy. Despite growing up in poverty, or maybe as a result of it, she had highly developed interpersonal skills. Daisy cared about the others in her class and was always first to notice if something was wrong with another child. During Daisy's first few dictated stories, she did her best to include everyone in the classroom within the stories she told. It was as if she was frightened about leaving anyone out in case it upset them. What better way is there to connect with the other children than by naming them in your story.

Daisy – age 4 (first story Reception)

There was a little boy called Ethan. And he lived in a house. And a little boy called Benji. And now there's a house. And Benji went into the house. And then a naughty horrible witch came into the house. And Gaia was in the house. And Tamara was in the house. And Mia, and Liam. And Timea. And Lance. And Milly. And Ollie. And Jason. And Alex. And Elouise.

Daisy would have included everyone in this story if we hadn't reached the bottom of the page. As she dictated each name, she looked around the room to see who she had missed. I explained that when we act out stories, we invite children to take on each character from where they sit around the stage. I reminded her that the names she used would not necessarily be the children who got to play those characters. Daisy was okay with that, and I used her story to introduce the rest of the class to the idea of pretending to be another child. The names were our characters. The children were actors pretending to be them.

Daisy's first story is not an amazing narrative. Here is an only child, who has no one to play with at home, and whose knowledge of story and story structure is limited. In this situation, of course, her early stories won't have the richness of children like Ethan or Ava, who have been listening to stories from birth. Daisy hasn't got the experience to know how to move a story forward. However, even within this simple narrative we can see the same intuitive understanding of story structure that is present in the stories of other young children.

Daisy introduces two characters, Ethan and Benji. It is unclear which one of them is the hero, but there is more suspense around the part of the story where Benji is involved. "And Benji went into the house." This feels like a Call to Adventure.

"And then a naughty, horrible witch comes in." Now we have our second story ingredient. The danger has arrived. Something is about to go wrong. These rudimentary building blocks are instinctive even in children who haven't heard many stories. However, having set up the premise – two boys in a house with a horrible witch, Daisy didn't know how to develop her story further. As a result, she moved on to something that she did understand – how to make others feel included.

Daisy's constant questioning, the way she pushes at the rules, and her curiosity about everyone in her class provides her with a great skill. This is not in an academic way, but in her understanding of group dynamics, of what makes people tick, of how to subvert a situation to get what she wants.

Having seen other children's stories acted out, Daisy realised that one of the benefits of this activity was that she could get everyone on the stage together if only she could get me to agree to it. But her page was full, and there were still more children she hadn't named. Daisy needed a different approach and fast. Just as we were about to act out her first story, Daisy changed the ending.

"There's a bit more," she said, pointing to the bottom of the page.

"Go on," I said, curious to know where this was going.

"And then everyone came into the house," continued Daisy. "I need the whole class in there."

The smile that she hadn't yet learned to hide, the one that revealed she knew exactly what she was doing, crept across her face. Of course, I let her get away with it. As we acted Daisy's story, all the children took it in turn to step onto the stage and pretend to go into the house. This smart way of bending the rules, of making sure no one was left out, won Daisy a place in my heart.

It was the first term in Reception, and the difference between children who had heard lots of stories and those who had heard far fewer was beginning to show. Daisy stayed by my side whenever I scribed for anyone else, listening curiously to everything they said. When I performed my oral storytelling session at the start of each of my visits, Daisy would sit as close as she could to me, closing her eyes so she could picture every word. Where stories were concerned, Daisy was a sponge, and in the second story she dictated, Daisy demonstrated her growing understanding of narrative.

Daisy – age 4 (second story Reception)

There was a boy called Benji. And Tamara was knocking on the door of Benji's house. And Ariel was in Benji's house. And Belle. And Liam wanted to go in the house. And Raya is in the house. And Ethan. And Timea. They were playing in the treehouse. And Lance and Alison and Henry. And the treehouse popped. And it popped like a balloon. And it floats in the air.

Before Daisy told this story, I advised her that if we had all the children on the stage, it might be hard to do the acting. I reminded her that when we did her story last time, there wasn't much room to move. As Daisy began to dictate the list of names, I wondered if she'd listened to me. Then her face changed. It was as if she'd pictured something in her mind and had to share it with me. There was an urgency to her speech as she blurted out, "And the treehouse popped."

Daisy had paid attention to what I'd said about the stage being too full, and halfway through her dictation, she'd found a creative way to incorporate this into her story. Suddenly she was off. For the first time since I'd met her, Daisy stopped looking around to see what everyone else was doing and dived into the world of her story. It was as if her creative Genius had entered the room and was whispering in her ear. Then, out of nowhere came a simile. "And it popped like a balloon." Embracing this image, Daisy imagined the house floating away. The art of improvisation is about taking one idea and following it to its furthest reaches. From the moment the house became too full, Daisy began to improvise.

During the acting out, Daisy shouted the word BANG as the treehouse popped, and all of the children, including Daisy, were thrown across the stage. "Pretend you've been thrown out the treehouse, and you're lying on the floor."

As the house floated away, Daisy gathered the children into a circle so that they could fly off together. Timea stayed where she was, lying on the floor. But Daisy noticed. She reached out a hand. "You need to come with us. We're flying away." Helping Timea to her feet, Daisy made sure she was included.

By the Spring Term of Reception, Daisy was beginning to tell stories with more of a clear through-line.

Daisy – age 5 (Reception)

There was a little girl called Belle. She lived in a house with no anybody to play with. And she cried and cried forever. And for ages and ages and ages. She went to her grandma's. She runned from the big bad wolf and the bear.

Sometimes it was as if Daisy's stories were long pieces of string, with one thought jumping to the next. Belle had no one to play with. Therefore she cried. Tears led to being taken to Grandma's to be looked after. Going to Grandma's equals thoughts of Little Red Riding Hood. That story involves a wolf. Wolves and bears were joined together in many of this class's stories, so the bear gets a mention too. The end.

Around this time, Daisy stopped using the other children's names in her stories and began to include a character named Belle. The name is borrowed from the Disney version of Beauty and the Beast. Daisy also began to include references to the emotions she felt about being an only child. "She lived in a house with no anybody to play with. And she cried and cried forever." Daisy desperately wanted someone to play with at home. She often spoke about how much she wanted a brother or a sister "like everyone else."

But Daisy's stories weren't just about these emotions. She also knew how to play to her audience, to provoke a reaction from them. At a time when toilets were the height of five-year-old humour, Daisy told a story about them. Toilets made the other children laugh, and Daisy liked getting a response. It was bound to happen.

Daisy – age 5 (Reception)

Once upon a time, there was a little girl. And she went down the toilet. And she was trying to get out, but she can't breathe. And she just runned away from the big bear.

In this story, Daisy shows us the depth of her creative thinking. Her hero accepts the Call to Adventure and goes down the toilet. But it wasn't just for comic effect. Daisy tells us what it was like down there, "but she can't breathe."

During the acting out, Daisy mimed being squashed in the pipes. In order to portray this clearly, Daisy must have imagined what it would be like to go down a toilet. That is an incredible feat of imagination.

The end of this story seems to jump from being down a toilet to running from a big bear. However, this isn't such a big gap when you see the story being acted out. Daisy, in the role of the little girl, wriggled out the pipe and looked around frantically before running from the bear. Watching how Daisy took on this role, it was possible to fill in the gaps and imagine her popping out of the toilet pipe into a strange new world where bears are enormous. This is a portal story – rather than just going down the toilet, Daisy travelled through it.

Towards the end of her year in Reception, Daisy told the following story.

Daisy – age 5 (Reception)

There was a little girl called Belle. She lived in a village, and she lived in a cottage. And she had a father and three sisters. And there was a mum, and she said, "It's dinner time." And they gone to bed. And when they four gone to bed, Mother read a story to them. And when they wake up, they have breakfast. And they had Weetabix.

This story of family bliss was far removed from Daisy's own life. Here was Daisy's perfect family; three sisters, a doting father and a mother who reads stories. When the story was acted out, Daisy and the three pretend sisters lay down to sleep in a house made out of children. The father sat beside them while Mother read a story.

Shakespeare's Hamlet says, "The purpose of playing, was and is, to hold as 'twere the mirror up to nature." But with Daisy, we go through the looking glass, and rather than showing us her world as it is, she shows it to us as she wants it to be. Daisy's growth as a storyteller is different from Ethan's. Where he was exposed to a rich variety of stories from an early age and has a readymade audience of parents to listen to him, Daisy has to discover it all as she goes along. The stories she shares are deeply personal. Rather than having a wide variety of stories and characters to choose from, her source material is her life. But Daisy is finding her voice, and her teachers have noticed and are amazed at how far she has come.

In Chapter 6, I listed the seven basic plot types. I haven't had many Rags to Riches stories from children I've scribed for, but as Daisy moved into her second term in Year 1, many of the stories she told fitted this model perfectly. Children brought up in poverty often have a greater awareness of the need for money. They know that their parent can't afford things and recognise what money can do. In her fairy tale way, Daisy told stories that showed how she saw the world and, more importantly, how she'd like to change it.

Daisy – age 6 (Year 1)

One lonely girl was in the forest, and she didn't have a home. And no food. Then she was walking, and she met a man, and he was nice. He said, "Do you want to come to my home?" And she said, "Yes."

Daisy – age 6 (Year I)

One little girl was walking in a forest. She had a ripped dress, and she couldn't afford a house because she didn't have any money. And she saw a prince coming by. And she fell into a pond. And the prince grabbed her out of the pond, and dragged her to the castle. And then she woke up, and the Prince wanted to ask her, "Will you marry me". And she said "yes".

Daisy – (Year 2)

Once upon a time, there was a girl walking through the woods. She had nowhere to stay, and she didn't have any money. She found someone in the woods that was chasing after her. And that was a bear and a wolf. And then someone nice came into the woods that did have a home, and they did have money. And then the little girl went home with them.

The stories above were told by Daisy during her time in Year 1 and Year 2. There are also many others stories that follow the same theme. The similarities are striking. In each story, the girl has no money, no home, no food and is always in the woods or the forest. Also, there is always someone nice who takes her to his house, rounding off the story with a happy ending.

During the time I worked with Daisy, she would often talk about her Mum's new boyfriend, how she hoped they'd get married, and how much she wanted a brother or a sister. Using a fairy tale genre, Daisy tells us about her life and shows us what she most desires. Helicopter Stories offered her a place to try out this alternate reality.

Throughout this publication, I have looked at the growth of many storytellers as they start out on their hero's journey. But when I look back at Daisy, I realise she has already completed one arc of her story. In the three years I knew her, she grew from a child who needed to include everyone in her stories to someone who was beginning to reflect on her own story and how she would like her world to be – a perfect story arc.

Daisy didn't have the start in life that some children have, but by regularly having an audience, by being listened to and valued, she began to create stories that connected her with others. This is what storytelling is all about. Theatre attracted me in the same way Helicopter Stories attracted Daisy because we both had a story we needed to share and a desire to find our voice.

I have no doubt that Daisy will continue to get into trouble just like I did. She is still rebellious and will always have that spark that is at times frustrating and at other times endearing. But hopefully, the confidence she has developed over the past three years, alongside the belief in herself as a storyteller that I didn't find until I was much older, will serve her well through the rest of her journey.

8 The Return of the Storytellers

"A fact by itself may open a door to the castle, but if we place the fact into a story, unforeseen tunnels are revealed as we crisscross and mingle and expand our horizons."

Vivian Gussin Paley
(Looking for magpie: Another Voice in the Classroom)

DOI: 10.4324/9781003161400-9

Crossing the Threshold

It was Thursday 1 July 2021 when I pulled into the school car park. I took a deep breath, put on my mask and walked into the entrance hall. I passed the temperature test at the door and made my way to the empty classroom. I sat on the floor and waited, glad to be back but feeling the strangeness of it all. It wasn't long before I heard a bustle outside, and the door flew open. The children peered in, smiling, inquisitively, taller than when I'd seen them last. I'd taped a stage on the floor before they arrived, and to my joy, they sat around it, just like they used to.

Tests, Allies and Enemies

"Hi," I said when they were all seated. I told them how pleased I was to be back. How I'd missed them and that I wanted to know how they'd been. There was silence for a moment. Then slowly, these children, now eight years old, who I had worked with so regularly since they were four, whose stories of the last eighteen months I had missed out on due to Covid-19, gradually began to open up to me.

The children updated me on their new pets, the rabbits and hamsters, budgies, and bulldogs that had entered their lives. If it hadn't been for Covid, these animals would have featured in the stories they dictated or the anecdotes they shared with me whenever I was in their class. These true-life stories are how we connect with each other. In oral storytelling traditions, when a tribe ceases to tell a story, part of that cultural knowledge is lost. This was how I felt seated around that taped-out stage, aware that I had lost so much of my cultural knowledge of these children who I'd once known so well. By sharing their stories with me, they welcomed me back into their tribe, ensuring I was up-to-date on all their important moments.

I'd not been there long when Tamara told me about Benji's dog, and Alex told me about his goldfish, both of which had died recently. The room fell silent, and we paused to reflect on all the pets we had lost.

Then came the good news. Alison had become an aunty even though she was only eight, and Daisy, whose dream of having a younger sibling featured so heavily in her stories, burst with excitement as she told me of the birth of her baby brother. Her joy reminded me of how often she's spoken about being alone, and I wished I'd been there to share in her delight when she found out that her mum was having a baby.

Once I'd caught up on everyone's lives, I told the children the purpose of my trip. I wanted to find out what they remembered about Helicopter Stories and what they thought of it now. I handed them their individual Helicopter Stories book containing all the stories they had told, drawn, or written since they were four years old. The children cheered as I took these out of my bag, delighted to be reunited with the stories from their past. Soon the room was full of reading and giggling and voices saying, "I remember this," and "Oh, I can't read this bit," and "Is that my writing?"

Approach to the Inmost Cave

I put on some classical music, and for a while, the children read in silence until Hannah screeched, "Oh my word, what is this? There was a princess. I wrote a story about a princess. This is so weird."

Suddenly, all the children joined in, wanting to share the astonishment and humour of what they were reading.

"I have a dinosaur in my story," said Benji. "And a dragon."

"Once there was a little girl called Alison," read Milly. "You're in my book Alison. I can't believe I wrote a story about you."

The children began to flick through their stories, amazed at how often they had included each other's names.

"And when we acted it out," said Milly, "we had to pretend to be each other."

Noah burst out laughing. "And I always ended up being you," he said.

The Ordeal

"Look, Lance's in one of my stories," said Jason, suddenly. He didn't usually talk that much so hearing him speak was a surprise. Then I remembered how close he was with Lance. The room fell silent. Lance had moved house just before Covid-19, and there were other children who had left the school in the three years I'd been working there.

"Ethan's in this story," said Benji, pointing to a page in his book.

"And here's Elouise," said Tamara

"It's so weird looking back," said Alison, "because a lot of people have left, and they were in my stories. They were my friends."

"They were in my stories too," said Hannah.

We paused for a while to remember friends who were no longer there. Some of the children called out their names, Lance, Ethan, Gaia, Ollie, Elouise, a roll call of the departed. It was as if the power contained in these stories enabled us to summon up their spirits and welcome them back to the tribe. I was sure I could sense them in the room.

Then the moment passed.

Reward

"How does it feel seeing your old Helicopter Stories books after all this time?" I asked, keen to see if the children could articulate the emotions they were experiencing.

"Weird," said Daisy. "I haven't seen this book in a while, and I think things have changed over the past year."

We all nodded sagely. Things had certainly changed. We had been through a global pandemic that was still ongoing; the children had been locked down, schooled at home, spent months where they weren't allowed to see members of their own family. And during that time, we'd all grown older.

"It brings back memories of when I was littler," said Benji. "I feel like I am in Year 1 again, more than in Year 3. Looking through my stories is like looking at what I did in Reception."

"It reminds me of how little I was. What I used to like and what made me laugh," said Liam.

"We made up these stories ages ago," said Mia. "It's funny like it's about our lives."

"Like history," said Tamara.

"It is history," I said. "Your history and it reminds you of the things you used to like, the things that were important to you."

"I must have liked Pokémon so much…" said Alex. "I've already found seven stories with them in. Me and Liam wrote so many stories with Pokémon in." He smiled as he remembered. "And then one day we found another idea, Minecraft."

Liam nodded. Between the two of them, there were so many stories about Minecraft. These stories connected these two boys, giving them the passion to write pages and pages on each of my weekly visits. Allowing two boys, who would not typically be seen writing, to sit side by side for over an hour and craft the words of a story that meant so much to them.

And then there were the older children who came in to scribe the children's stories.

"On 1st March 2018, Robert, my buddy from Year 6, came in, and he wrote the words to my story. I remember telling it to him and him laughing," said Alison. "I liked Robert. He always laughed at my stories."

Vivian Gussin Paley – Personal Correspondence

There are few places where the roles we play can be better examined than on a stage. Their every innovation highlights and connects the individual voice to a communal spirit of fairness and friendship.

Observing children at play, one becomes aware of the basic issues of fairness being worked out by even the youngest students. The "social justice" message is strong when all the children in the group may tell their own stories and give equal opportunity to others to enter the plot of the ongoing drama.

The Road Back

Looking back over their old Helicopter Stories books gave each of these children so much to remember. What an incredible opportunity to be able to re-read your own words, revisiting how your voice sounded when you were four or five years old. As I listened to the children, I remembered seeing so many of them making their first mark on a page or scrambling to grab a pen and paper so they could write their own story on a week when it was not their turn to dictate. Now here they were, reflecting on their stories with sophistication and wonder. Writers sharing their work.

Liam's attention turned to his handwriting. He had been one of the most prolific writers in his class, so it was hardly surprising that he began to focus on this as he reached the stories he'd written himself.

"My writing is much neater now than it was," he laughed.

"I can't read my writing at all," said Alex.

There was a pause. Then Noah spoke. "When you came in, I really enjoyed writing stories, but I hate it now. When we did it with you, we did it for fun."

Resurrection

Noah's words snapped me out of the joy of reminiscing. They reminded me of the pressures the curriculum places on these children and how the obsession with testing and getting things right leaves little room for creativity. In 2006, Ken Robinson delivered his famous TED talk, "Do Schools Kill Creativity." As Noah spoke, I could sense his joy for telling stories dying. We cannot let this happen to our children.

In Helicopter Stories, when children choose to dictate or write their stories, they do it for themselves; they understand the reason they are doing it. Each story is placed in front of an audience. It has a purpose, and it has an end result. Writing for a purpose is such an important criterion. But, as Noah's comment highlights, this is often lost in an overcrowded curriculum. His remarks made me feel even more strongly that we must not let this pressure to write, to be grammatically correct, to structure children's writing in a way that is easier to mark and less enjoyable to create, we cannot let this get in the way of our children's growth as a storyteller.

When children dictate their stories, they share their imagination with their audience and see their words immortalized on the page.

> I love making my own imagination and telling it to you. You can read them back as you get older and write them again, and share them with your friends.
>
> (Hannah, age eight)

When children act out their stories, they make decisions about the way a character moves.

> When a story is acted out, I keep on seeing it in my head, even if I don't have my book with me, cos I've seen it on the stage. Sometimes what I imagine in my head is different when others act it out. It's not always what I expected. But I like seeing what others do with it.
>
> (Liam, age eight)

When acting in someone else's story, children listen intently, so they know what they have to do.

> When it's not my story, I like finding out what happens next and then acting that bit out.
>
> (Benji, age eight)

And finally, children get to be audience members and watch the stories of their peers.

> Helicopter Stories is like a movie, but it's shorter, and there's loads of them. And seeing it is exciting. You keep finding a new way to do something and are learning from others for your own stories.
>
> (Mia, age eight)

The quotes from the children above demonstrate how sophisticated their thinking has become about what makes a storyteller. These eight-year-olds grew up telling stories every week from their first week in Reception at age four. They know that stories are things you share with your friends, that you can see them in your head, and that they change when you bring them to life on a stage. They have discovered time and time again the joy of finding out what happens next. They realise that their stories are like tiny movies that are constantly changing and where there is always the chance to learn something new. I look around the stage and feel privileged to have shared a part of their hero's journey with each of them, to have been allowed to walk alongside them for a while and to witness the development of their natural storytelling abilities.

Children come into our schools and pre-schools as incredibly creative beings, eager to play, to explore and to take risks. We must not stifle this.

Return with the Elixir

As the conversation drew to an end, Benji stood up.

"Looking back," he said, "it's been so long since we've done this. I think it's been good seeing our stories. It's like the first time all over again."

Daisy looked at everyone sitting around the stage, and with a pained look on her face she said. "Doing everything we've done, having Helicopter Stories in our lives, it feels really good. I don't want it to stop. I feel like everyone has a different attitude when we do it, and it's fun. Just thinking about never doing it again makes me sad."

"Well, maybe, if you like," I replied. "Perhaps we could act out some of your old stories now."

And, of course, everyone agreed.

With Thanks...

This book has been forming in my head for a long time but I would never have been able to write it without the help of the following people. My sister Lors, for sharing stories with me, that were whispered and giggled across the gap between our beds in the dark of night. To Bill, my husband, friend, administrator, cook, cheerleader, supporter and so much more, who is always ready to stop what he is doing and to read and comment on my latest chapter. To my son, Callum, who is never short of an encouraging word, and who has always been my motivation for why story is important. Amie Taylor for designing yet another stunningly beautiful cover, and for being able to capture the true essence of this publication through the cut-out images she positioned on a bridge. Elaine Bennett for doing me the honour of writing a foreword that had the ability to make me cry. Isla Hill, my business companion, comrade, friend and partner in crime, whose constant support and passion for this work is something I will never take for granted. Debby Thacker, board member, friend, and online mentor who has always been there during this lockdown writing process. Her thoughts and advice encouraged me to keep digging deeper and thinking harder as I explored the growth of a storyteller. Jane Katch, friend and advisor, who I have admired for years and who filled me with joy with her willingness to read and comment on those early versions of this work. Sheridan Upton, Lisa Wilkins, Faye Rogers and Amy Holt from St Paul's Primary School for their constant belief in the value of Helicopter Stories, and for allowing me to share my practice in their classrooms. And to Emma Williams and Vicky Strange at The Oaks Pre-school for always welcoming me into their setting and for allowing me to spend time with their wonderful children. Yvonne Robinson from Falkirk and Amanda Belbin from Bincombe Valley Nursery for sending me videos so I could transcribe their children. Emily, Harry and Samuel for one of my favourite photos. And to all the children and the adults and schools and settings who have helped by welcoming me or sending me their thoughts on what Helicopter Stories means to them and on why Vivian Gussin Paley is so important. Thank you to all of you for making this possible...

Bibliography

Books by Vivian Gussin Paley

Paley, Vivian G. (1979) *White Teacher*. Cambridge, MA: Harvard University Press. (Third edition published in 2000.)

—— (1981) *Wally's Stories: Conversations in the Kindergarten*. Cambridge, MA: Harvard University Press.

—— (1984) *Boys and Girls: Superheroes in the Dolls Corner*. Chicago: University of Chicago Press.

—— (1986) *Mollie is Three: Growing up in School*. Chicago: University of Chicago Press.

—— (1988) *Bad Guys Don't Have Birthdays: Fantasy Play at Four*. Chicago: University of Chicago Press.

—— (1990) *The Boy Who Would Be a Helicopter: The Uses of Storytelling in the Classroom*. Cambridge, MA: Harvard University Press.

—— (1992) *You Can't Say You Can't Play*. Cambridge, MA: Harvard University Press.

—— (1995) *Kwanzaa and Me: A Teacher's Story*. Cambridge, MA: Harvard University Press.

—— (1997) *The Girl with the Brown Crayon*. Cambridge, MA: Harvard University Press.

—— (1999) *The Kindness of Children*. Cambridge, MA: Harvard University Press.

—— (2001) *In Mrs Tully's Room: A Childcare Portrait*. Cambridge, MA: Harvard University Press.

—— (2004) *A Child's Work: The Importance of Fantasy Play*. Chicago: The University of Chicago Press.

—— (2010) T*he Boy on The Beach: Building Community Through Play*. Chicago: University of Chicago Press.

Other Works by Vivian Gussin Paley

Paley, Vivian G. (1995). "Looking for Magpie: Another Voice in the Classroom." In Hunter McEwan and Kieron Egan (Eds.), *Narrative in Teaching, Learning, and Research* (pp. 91–99). New York: Teachers College Press.

MakeBelieve Arts

MakeBelieve Arts are a UK-based registered charity (https://makebelievearts.co.uk)

MakeBelieve Arts Online Learning

https://helicopterstories.co.uk/online-learning/

■ Helicopter Stories On Demand

■ The Poetry Basket

■ The Story Basket

Princesses, Dragons and Helicopter Stories: Storytelling and Story Acting in the Early Years is a "how to" on the Helicopter Stories approach.

Secondary Publications

Bettelheim, Bruno. (1976) *The Uses of Enchantment – The meaning and importance of fairytales.* London: Penguin Books.
Booker, Christopher. (2007) *The Seven Basic Plots – Why we tell stories.* London: Continuum Books.
Bottrill, Greg. (2018) *Can I Go and Play Now – rethinking the early years.* London: Sage Publications.
Brooks, Larry. (2011) *Story Engineering – Mastering the 6 core competences of successful writing.* Ontario: Writer's Digest Books.
Bruce, Tina, McNair, Lynn, Whinnett, Jane. (2020) *Putting Storytelling and the Heart of Early Childhood Practice – A reflective guide for early years practitioners.* Abingdon: Routledge.
Bruner, Jerome. (1985) *Child's Talk – Learning to use language.* New York: Norton.
Campbell, Joseph. (2012) *The Hero with a Thousand Faces.* 3rd ed. Novato, CA: New World Library.
Chukovsky, Kornei. (1933) *From Two to Five.* Trans. Miriam Morton. Los Angeles: University of California Press.
Chukovsky, Kornei. (1974) *From Two to Five.* Berkeley: University of California Press.
Conkbayir, Mine. (2019) *Early Childhood and Neuroscience – Theory, research and implications for practice.* London: Bloomsbury Accademic.
Crago, Hugh. (2016) *Entranced by Story – Brain, tale and teller, from infancy to old age.* New York: Routledge.
Cron, Lisa. (2012) *Wired for Story – The Writer's Guide to using brain science to hook readers from the very first sentence.* New York: Ten Speed Press.
Dunbar, Robin. (1996) *Grooming, Gossip and the Evolution of Language.* London: Faber and Faber.
Fox, Carol. (1993) *At the Very Edge of the Forest – The influence of literature on storytelling by children.* London: Cassell.
Gottschall, Jonathan. (2013) *The Storytelling Animal – How stories make us human.* New York: Mariner Books.
Gove, Michael. (2013, 26 February) *Question Time,* BBC, Uxbridge.
Harari, Yuval Noah. (2014) *Sapiens – A brief history of humankind.* London: Vintage Books.

Harris, Paul L. (2000) *The Work of the Imagination*. Malden, MA: Blackwell Publishing.

Haven, Kendall. (2007) *Story Proof – The science behind the startling power of story*. Westport, CT: Libraries Unlimited.

Haven, Kendall. (2014) *Story Smart – Using the science of story to persuade, influence, inspire and teach*. Santa Barbara, CA: Libraries Unlimited.

Isaacs, Susan. (1946) *The Nursery Years – The mind of the child from birth to six years*. London: Routledge.

Jenkinson, Sally. (2001) *The Genius of Play – Celebrating the spirit of childhood*. Stroud: Hawthorn Press.

Jones, Gerard. (2002) *Killing Monsters – Why children need fantasy, super heroes and make-believe violence*. New York: Basic Books.

Kornberger, Horst. (2013) *The Power of Stories – Nurturing children's imagination and consciousness*. Edinburgh: Floris Books.

Lee, Trisha. (2016) *Princesses, Dragons and Helicopter Stories – Storytelling and story acting in the early years*. Abingdon: Routledge.

Palmer, Sue. (2020) *Play Is the Way, Child Development – Early years and the future of Scottish education*. Paisley: CCWB Press.

Sartre, Jean-Paul. (1988) *"What is literature?" and other essays*. Cambridge, MA: Harvard University Press.

Storr, Will. (2019) *The Science of Storytelling*. London: William Collins Books.

Sutton-Smith, Brian. (1981) *The Folkstories of Children*. Philadelphia PA: University of Pennsylvania Press.

Tatar, Maria. (2009) *Enchanted Hunters – The power of stories in childhood*. New York: W. W. Norton.

Twain, Mark. (2010 [1924]) *Mark Twain's Own Autobiography*. Madison, WI: University of Wisconsin Press

Weir, Ruth Hirsch. (1962) *Language in the Crib*. The Hague, NL: Mouton and Co.

Wolf, Maryanne. (2008) *Proust and the Squid – The story and science of the reading brain*. London: Icon Books.

Yorke, John. (2014) *Into the Woods – How stories work and why we tell them*. London: Penguin Books.

Online Videos

Abbott and Costello. (1940) *Who's on First*. USA: https://youtube.com/watch?v=kTcRRaXV-fg

Bloom, Paul. (2013) Paul Bloom, Yale University, speaks on the topic of Just Babies. Oxford: https://youtube.com/watch?v=MLrzetNHAYo

Gilbert, Elizabeth. (2009) Ted Talk. *Your Elusive Creative Genius*. California: https://ted.com/talks/elizabeth_gilbert_your_elusive_creative_genius

Hasson, Uri. (2016) Ted Talk. *This Is Your Brain on Communication*. Vancouver: https://ted.com/talks/uri_hasson_this_is_your_brain_on_communication?language=en

Haven, Kendall. (2015) *Your Brain on Story*. Stanford, CA: https://youtube.com/watch?v=zGrf0LGn6Y4

Phillips, David JP. (2017) Ted Talk. *The Magical Science of Storytelling*. Stockholm, Sweden: https://youtube.com/watch?v=Nj-hdQMa3uA

Robinson, Ken. (2006) Ted Talk. *Do Schools Kill Creativity?* Monterey, CA: www.ted.com/talks/sir_ken_robinson_do_schools_kill_creativity?language=en

Storr, Will. (2018) Ted Talk. *The Science of Storytelling*. Manchester, UK: https://ted.com/talks/will_storr_the_science_of_storytelling

Online Articles

Bring Back the Bedtime Story. (2017)
https://southparade.wakefield.sch.uk/bring-back-bedtime-stories/
https://booktrust.org.uk/news-and-features/features/2017/april/bring-back-bedtime-stories-one-schools-campaign-to-get-kids-reading/
Cave Paintings. (2019)
https://nature.com/articles/d41586-019-03826-4 – oldest paintings
https://independent.co.uk/climate-change/news/archaeology-cave-art-drawings-indonesia-palaeolithic-animals-a9248886.html
Hearts Beat Together. (2017) https://ucl.ac.uk/pals/news/2017/nov/audience-members-hearts-beat-together-theatre
https://heraldscotland.com/news/15663737.heart-watching-live-theatre-unifies-audiences-heartbeats-research-finds/
Laura van der Erve, Senior Research Economist, Institute for Fiscal Studies. (2020) Quoted in a government press release: www.gov.uk/government/news/the-long-shadow-of-deprivation
Literacy Trust Research. (2019) https://literacytrust.org.uk/news/help-us-support-the-383775-children-who-dont-have-a-book-this-christmas/
Outdoor Play. (2012) https://bbc.co.uk/news/education-19065224
https://childinthecity.org/2018/01/15/children-spend-half-the-time-playing-outside-in-comparison-to-their-parents/?gdpr=accept
https://gov.uk/government/statistics/monitor-of-engagement-with-the-natural-environment-pilot-study-visits-to-the-natural-environment-by-children
The Next Chapter – Book Trust 2021 Strategy. (2021) https://cdn.booktrust.org.uk/globalassets/resources/misc/the_next_chapter_booktrust_strategy.pdf